THE JOY OF FINDING FISH

The *Joy* of Finding *FISH*

A Journey of Fulfilment, Inspiration, Success & Happiness

CHRISTOPHER MILLER

First published in 2022 by Hambone Publishing
Melbourne, Australia

Cover illustration by Cameron Miller
Editing by Mish Phillips and Lexi Wight
Typesetting and design by David W. Edelstein

For information about this title, contact:
Christopher Miller
chris@christophermiller.co.nz
https://christophermiller.co.nz

ISBN 978-1-922357-34-2 (paperback)
ISBN 978-1-922357-35-9 (ebook)

CONTENTS

ACKNOWLEDGEMENTS

I never expected to write a book, especially during one of the most difficult years of my life, and there are a number of important people who contributed to the process.

Ben, Mish, Lexi, David and the team at Hambone Publishing have been instrumental to keeping me on track with patient feedback and encouragement. They have guided me through the writing and publishing process with minimum stress or anxiety.

Antonia and Tash, I'm grateful for your loyalty and efforts to keep my practice alive through the last year, and for your proofreading and suggestions to improve the manuscript as it developed.

Frankie, for your contribution to chapter 3, and living your values so transparently.

Kate and Roisin, for your review of the manuscript and ensuring I honoured Fiona appropriately.

James N, for your professional listening and advice.

James B, for your incredible loyalty as a client and for role modelling FISH.

Mom, Dad, Nick, Amy and my extended Canadian family, thank you for offering an ear through challenging times and for your unconditional love and support.

Cameron, thank you for developing the concept for the cover art of this book, and for being the mature, independent young man you are. I am exceptionally proud of you. Many elements of this book were directly inspired by you.

Thanks also to Ross for your positive, upbeat personality.

And for Fiona, my never-ending source of fulfilment, inspiration, success and happiness, I will be grateful forever.

Foreword

I T'S TEMPTING, IN life, to be driven by the pursuit of a permanent state of being, one that says you've made it, one that gives your life meaning. For some, this aspired state is happiness. For others, success alone is their benchmark. Yet, such a narrow goal doesn't usually survive the ups and downs that we all experience through a lifetime. Are you really going to be happy all the time? Can you guarantee success in every endeavour? And, in not meeting your desired state of being, it's easy to become disillusioned and give up all together.

Over many years of exploration, I realised that instead, we should be focusing on a variety of states. Ones that support and complement each other but can equally exist when the others are not present. From this realisation came FISH – fulfilment, inspiration, success, happiness – and an everlasting journey to finding them in each moment.

I initially felt compelled to study wisdom literature explaining the process of achieving each of these states. Like many people before me, studying fulfilment, inspiration, success, and happiness felt like a continuous pursuit of a *better* me, a striving that might have been never-ending. However, a few profound personal crises disrupted my studying and led me to realise that just *being* was enough. This is what I should have been measuring – my ability to *be* fulfilled, *be* inspired, *be* successful, and *be* happy

– in any given moment. In time, I have realised that as much as you can study these states, nothing compares to experiencing them personally, and offering your example to the world.

In 2017, I began to measure my own experience of FISH by scoring days, weeks and months based on the following questions:

* On a scale of 1 to 10, how much did I live my purpose (fulfilment)? (And why?)
* On a scale of 1 to 10, how inspired did I feel? (About what, and why?)
* On a scale of 1 to 10, how successful did I feel? (And why?)
* On a scale of 1 to 10, how happy did I feel? (And why?)

I wasn't always consistent in my measuring but, over several years, I slowly put together a picture of my days, a pattern of how I felt about each of these four areas. What I learnt truly changed my approach to life, and helped me to take value out of even the most challenging of situations. Importantly, I realised that my answers to those four questions were more a choice about my state of mind than an absolute truth; even on a 'bad' day, I could identify events or insights that led me to rarely give a score below 7.

My bias, unsurprisingly, was to record the 10:10:10:10 days, as they were few and far between, and such a highlight of a life well-lived. Who wouldn't want to make a record of such days! Yet, even on a catastrophically bad day, like the day my wife was diagnosed with a brain tumour, I didn't score myself at 0:0:0:0. While success and happiness were indeed ranked at 0, my inspiration to take action was pretty strong, and my sense of purpose as a husband was off the charts. I have only ever recorded a handful of 0:0:0:0 days, mainly because I have rarely been separated from my family, which is an enormous source of fulfilment as a husband and a father.

I wholeheartedly believe that focusing on fulfilment, inspiration, success and happiness as a whole, rather than the pursuit of one state at the expense of others, is the pathway to a genuinely meaningful life. Life is nuanced and full, and measuring it by a broad and generous set of states allows for the ups, downs and sideways to be appreciated in their own way.

This book is my attempt to summarise the principles of FISH, and in many cases, my personal journey to discovering them for myself, along with family, friend, and client examples when compelling and relevant. This is not a scientific report, a treatise, or a textbook. The best way I have to explain the joy of finding FISH is through my own story, and thus this book walks the line between memoir, leadership development, and personal growth. The art of finding fulfilment, inspiration, success, and happiness is individual and personal for everyone. I am hopeful that some of the stories and patterns contained here will serve as a shortcut towards catching your own FISH.

You will notice that throughout the book I have asked the reader questions and left space for you to fill in an answer. I would invite you to treat this as a 'workbook' to get maximum value from the experience.

CHAPTER 1

Life Is A Rollercoaster

Run and you'll live — at least a while. And dying in
your beds many years from now, would you be willing
to trade all the days, from this day to that, for one
chance, just one chance, to come back here and tell
our enemies that they may take our lives, but they'll
never take our freedom!

William Wallace, *Braveheart*

U NTIL APRIL 2009, my life was blessed more than I ever could have imagined. On the surface, I was phenomenally successful, with high levels of academic and career achievements in Canada, the UK, and New Zealand. I met my best friend in 1997 and had the good sense to marry her in 2001. We had two amazing sons, born in 2003 and 2008 and, prior to our first crisis, were living the life of our dreams in Wellington, New Zealand.

Perhaps life was too easy, and I was meant to experience and navigate challenges that I never could have dreamed of. What I have since realised is that the extraordinary crises that my family and I experienced from 2009 to 2020 were hidden blessings, especially in the creation of fulfilment, inspiration, success, and happiness. Without them, I would never have fully understood the joy of finding FISH, and this book would never have come into existence. So, what was it that led me down this path? Where did it all start?

MY OWN DATE WITH DESTINY

In my pursuit of a better version of me, I had invested substantially in personal development, including three Anthony Robbins events in the UK and Australia. For those not familiar, Tony Robbins hosts high octane, multi-day processes that challenge you physically, mentally, and emotionally. The event *Unleash the Power Within* in London involved quite amazing confidence building exercises, including a 10-foot fire walk over hot coals.

This was extremely adrenalin inducing, but not even the most impactful exercise of the event. *Wealth Mastery* in Melbourne had a big focus on attracting wealth and, most importantly, defining what you want more of in life.

By my third time participating in one of his events (*Date with Destiny* in the Gold Coast, April 2009), I felt ready and poised to make a big breakthrough. My wife, on the other hand, was sceptical and mildly concerned by my state of mind and over-commitment to these life-changing events. In addition, our then five-year-old and six-month-old were in tow, with the bulk of the caregiving falling to my wife as I was in sessions all day for five days. In retrospect, my selfishness was off the charts.

Some of the processes at *Date with Destiny* included high energy goal setting, connecting to 'oneness', meditation, chakra activation, and powerful interactive exercises with thousands of other participants. I was *all in*, fully committed to each process without understanding the potential consequences. During one of the meditations, I believe I experienced a kundalini awakening, which is an energy process from the base of the spine right up to the crown of your head, much like lightning coursing up your body and exploding through the top of your head. It is difficult to articulate the significance of this experience, but it is an example of the physical as well as mental, emotional, and spiritual nature of the various experiences during *Date with Destiny*. In any case, I was highly susceptible to the power of suggestion, which led me down a dangerous rabbit hole.

By day three of the event, I was beginning to feel somewhat detached, and my delusions of grandeur were getting more unusual and extreme. Stimulated by the oneness experiences, I believe I experienced "God-consciousness", which was extraordinary and highly overwhelming. In the evenings after the event, my wife was having trouble keeping me grounded or engaging me with the family in any meaningful way. Day four led to more stimulating activities and inspiring content from the stage, all of which contributed to more delusions. At one point, these delusions led me to stand on my chair and yell gibberish at Tony, who was on the stage at the time, just to get his attention. Various people at the event got me out of the room and backstage, where I was fed and watered and sent back to my hotel for sleep. My mind continued to race, and I was only able to control my thinking for short periods of time.

The following day, we set off for Brisbane from the Gold Coast, and my behaviour in the car was becoming dangerously erratic, including rapidly changing from deep sleep to aggressively awake, throwing water around the car, and articulating very odd dreams to my wife, who was driving. Upon arrival at Brisbane airport, I bolted from the car and rushed into the terminal, completely out of control. I was tackled by security and handcuffed until paramedics could arrive and take me to a Brisbane hospital where I spent five days in a mental health ward, very little of which has remained in my memory. Given my wife's inability to see me or contribute to my care at the time, she and the boys returned to New Zealand, leaving me in Australia until I recovered sufficiently to be able to fly home. The five days in a mental health ward, drugged for my own safety and that of others, are my only 0:0:0:0 days, especially given that I could not function as a father or a husband during that time. Discharged on an anti-psychotic, and newly diagnosed as bipolar, I somehow managed to navigate my way through international travel. I returned to Wellington in a stable but fragile state of mind.

GROWTH AND UNDERSTANDING

From 2009 to 2013, I was in a battle to come to terms with my diagnosis, and find the right balance of mood stabiliser and anti-psychotic to create a "normal" way of life. My connection to my wife Fiona, and to the boys, was profound, and they were often literally my lifeline as I experienced short and extended periods of depression, anxiety, and elevated moods. The best way to describe managing a bipolar mental health condition would be to imagine happy and sad days, and then magnify them hundredfold, never really sure which end of the spectrum you might experience on any given day. Around this time, I also transitioned from my dream job as a Wellington business coach to a consultant position with a global management consultancy firm (Gallup), signs that my self-preservation and my talent were strong enough to seek out and secure a stable role that I was capable of delivering under very challenging personal circumstances.

Since 2013, my stability and self-confidence regarding my condition have improved every year, and my delivery as a senior consultant and executive coach has continued to thrive. By 2017, my desire to do something creative for myself led me to exit Gallup as an employee and establish a coaching and mentoring practice, serving small business owners in New Zealand, and offering mentoring to CliftonStrengths coaches around the world on how to set up businesses for themselves, or lift their ability to facilitate strengths-based organisations.

A SECOND GREAT DISASTER

Three years into my own professional practice, disaster struck the Miller family once more. While I had thought that my five days in a mental health ward were the worst days of my life, they didn't compare to June of 2020. As a family, we had coped with the Covid-19 pandemic fairly well, operating work and school from home with many joyful moments along the way. On the 8th of June, the day New Zealand lowered its Covid-19 status from alert level 2 to alert level 1, Fiona collapsed at home. We rushed to the emergency department at Wellington Hospital where she was investigated and scanned, leading to the discovery of a lesion, essentially a tumour, in the right hemisphere of her brain. The day after her admission, Fiona's condition deteriorated significantly; she wasn't able to eat, or even hold normal conversations due to confusion and lethargy. That evening, I had the surreal and heart-stopping experience of being shown Fiona's brain scans, revealing what appeared to be a ping-pong sized tumour in her head. With little to contribute to her care, I left Fiona and picked up our sons from diving practice. After making small talk with other diving parents, I got the boys home for dinner. I felt numb, but absolutely committed to helping Fiona through whatever options became available and assisting the boys to understand what was happening.

Wednesday the 10th of June saw Fiona stabilise and get stronger, which gave her surgeons confidence to proceed with brain surgery the next day. Amazingly, they recommended and administered a contrast media (Gliolan), which helps highlight cancerous cells in the brain and assists with removing as much of the tumour as is possible. Gliolan is taken as a liquid orally and migrates to Glioblast cells in the brain, which are the source of the tumour. The surgeon is guided by the specific cells that are lit up, which helps differentiate between cancerous and healthy cells. One of the worst moments of my life was leaving her in pre-op on the day of her surgery, knowing that for over five hours, her life would be in the hands of her anaesthetists and surgeons. That evening, the surgical team used words like "routine", "uncomplicated", and "went better than expected" to describe her surgery, none of which I would have expected to be associated with brain surgery! Fiona's remarkable recovery began the evening of her surgery when she got back to her ward and started cracking jokes with the nursing team.

ROAD – OR POOL – TO RECOVERY

In the following three days, Fiona's independence and strength grew in leaps and bounds, and by Sunday June 14th we were traveling home as a family to care for her there. Our main concern was Fiona's ambition to push herself to do too much, especially given restrictions with using devices and any additional brain stimulation. Slowly but surely, Fiona re-integrated reading for pleasure, walks for fitness, sudoku, and small doses of television and time on her phone. Her passion for swimming meant that it would not be long before we would find ourselves in a local pool. As part of her navigation and recovery from radiation therapy, Fiona re-engaged with one of her favourite activities, long-distance swimming. Starting small, Fiona decided to embark on a charity swim for the Neurological Foundation of NZ by swimming the length of New Zealand (as the crow flies), or about 1402km! While her lengths in recovery began as low as 20 in a session, she built up her fitness and stamina over several months to an extraordinary 150 lengths in a single session.

Joy often feels intangible and difficult to articulate or measure, but November 30th was a day of pure joy for our family. That was the day that Fiona received the results of her post-surgical MRI scan, which, according to her oncologist, was "very clear", without even the expected inflammation around the surgery site. We left the hospital skipping and celebrated that evening with our favourite take-away. Having slept nearly five months with one eye on Fiona's health, December 2020 was one of the happiest and most restful periods for our family in a long time.

We were told at the outset that one of the potential consequences of brain surgery was seizures, and with over six months of stability post-surgery, we were hopeful and perhaps naïve that Fiona would not experience this side effect. On December 27th, while on holiday in Hanmer Springs, Fiona was swimming lengths when a seizure struck. I had the misfortune to approach the lap pool to check on Fiona only to find her unconscious and surrounded by four lifeguards. Unbelievably well-supported by the Hanmer Springs staff, a local GP, and St John Ambulance, Fiona was transported urgently to the Christchurch emergency department. While en route, Fiona suffered a second seizure. She was unconscious for approximately 30 minutes and semiconscious for approximately 12 hours while being cared for in Christchurch. The next day, Fiona was discharged on anti-seizure medication. On medical advice, we cancelled our South Island holiday to return to Wellington.

It is often said that every cloud has a silver lining, and our situation was no exception. As a result of cancelling our summer holiday early, we were able to pick up a new member of the family: our Viszla puppy, Talisker, one week early. She integrated into the family brilliantly and contributed greatly to Fiona's self-care and her ability to pace herself post-seizure.

Given the new concern, Fiona's oncologist recommended an MRI scan which detected that her tumour had returned in the same location, slightly bigger than it had been previously. Following various surgical and medical consultations, Fiona opted for a second brain surgery to have as much of the tumour removed as possible. A successful four-hour operation took place in mid-February 2021, and all but a very small trace of tumour tissue was removed. Fiona is now considering various chemotherapy options to suppress tumour growth and, as always, she'll make the decision balancing both quantity and quality of life.

BLESSINGS IN DISGUISE

While all of the above might sound like doom and gloom, or catastrophic events in the life of any family, I have come to realise that each and every moment has been a blessing in disguise. More than anything, the levels of resilience and calmness under pressure were extraordinary elements of each situation. My own strength, confidence, and self-management as a high-performing bipolar father, husband, and coach continues to be remarkable, and informs the way I help other leaders and individuals understand and navigate mental health conditions.

Fiona's robustness is unbelievable and, despite various knock-backs, she continues to live a life full of optimism and positive energy. She is a fantastic role model to so many people around her. Our sons, Cameron and Ross, have been with us every step of the way – from the chaotic car journey from the Gold Coast to Brisbane, to the pre- and post-op consultations with Fiona's surgeons, the boys have not missed or been omitted from a thing, and their quiet resilience has been a source of pride and amazement.

Remarkably, none of the above crises led to a FISH measure of 0:0:0:0, as one might expect. While some elements may drop to zero, our sense of purpose, sources of inspiration, definition of success, and moments of happiness may shine through even under the most difficult of circumstances.

Carpe diem – Seize the day.

CHAPTER 2

Creating Your Why

When we are no longer able to change a situation, we are challenged to change ourselves. Everything can be taken from a man but one thing: the last of the human freedoms—to choose one's attitude in any given set of circumstances, to choose one's own way. Between stimulus and response there is a space. In that space is our power to choose our response. In our response lies our growth and our freedom.

Viktor Frankl, *Man's Search for Meaning*

BEFORE WE READY our hook and line, we need the right kind of bait. Two things are absolutely vital to finding FISH – knowing what our purpose is and knowing what our values are. Without purpose, it is nearly impossible to find fulfilment and success (and even if you do, you may not recognise it). Without knowing your own values you'll likely have trouble identifying what makes you happy and inspired. Chapter 2 and Chapter 3 will delve deeply into these concepts, so that we come back to the rivers and oceans of our lives well-equipped for fishing.

Viktor Frankl's power to choose is an extraordinary concept that has the potential to influence every aspect of our lives. As I have explored the value and meaning of purpose, it has struck me that human beings are the only living things capable of conceiving, articulating, and living our purpose, however we choose. Indeed, we can choose to change our purpose every single day if it suits us.

What is curious is the concept of a higher purpose, perhaps one that is just out of reach of understanding. Whether you are atheist, agnostic, or deeply religious is irrelevant. You may not believe in a higher purpose at all, but that higher purpose may exist nonetheless.

UNDERSTANDING PURPOSE

Rod Hill, a wise coach and former CEO of Results.com, often shared a terrific metaphor for better understanding purpose. Imagine a honeybee, going about its business – flying, navigating, collecting pollen, cross-pollenating flowers, creating a hive, serving the queen – these are all the things that a bee **does** as part of its existence. But in the bigger picture, a bee's higher purpose is to **regenerate life**. The whole ecosystem of the world is dependent on the bee's existence. Now, imagine if every individual bee understood and grasped the responsibility of their higher purpose. Would they curl up in a ball under the sheer weight of their burden, or would they rise to the challenge? The fact that they do not understand the scale of their contribution to the world allows them to function through their daily life, by doing rather than bee-ing.

And so it is with most of humanity. Most people have rarely reflected on their purpose, or, if they have, it has been a flashing thought during a powerful moment of reflection, often ·soon to be forgotten. Perhaps this is our own safety mechanism as, similar to the bee, if we truly understood the significance of our higher purpose, we might not get out of bed in the morning!

For 38 years of my life, I had little conscious connection to my own purpose. I lived a life of achievement, moving from one academic, sporting, financial, or career goal to another, with little reflection about **why** I chose certain things over others. I was brought up sharply by a personal development event that fundamentally wired me to think about fulfilment and living your purpose first before identifying the strategies for success.

A SERIES OF WHYS

Following the dramatic events outlined in Chapter 1, and being confronted with a bipolar mental health diagnosis, I took to journaling a great deal to capture my thoughts and "sort out" my head as best I could. The impact of these events caused me to question myself and my existence – why me? Why now? Why my family? How do I navigate this? How do I define myself differently now? How do I survive? Thriving was a very distant point on the horizon.

The first question was the most profound: why me? I drafted hundreds of answers to that question, but there was only one that came back over and over again: because I can. Somehow, I had built a life and a safety net around me that allowed me to experience a catastrophe of soul that not many people have the privilege to discover. The turmoil of the earliest months post-crisis were an avalanche of insights and rapid thinking, some crazy, most interesting, and a few useful. These insights laid the groundwork for this book, and many other coaching interventions I use with my clients every single day.

Expanding on "Why me?", I was also curious to answer some of the following:

* What is my purpose?
* Why do I exist?
* What am I here to contribute?
* Why am I here?
* What "dent" would I like to leave in the universe? (Inspired by Steve Jobs.)
* What would I like my legacy to be?

What I love about these questions is the variety of perspectives that you can take. For example, do I mean what is my purpose *today*, or *in this lifetime*? What am I here to contribute – to work, to family, to community, to the world? The choice is entirely mine.

KNOWING WHY I EXIST

These questions led to the creation of my first meaningful purpose statement: "To be a great dad, loving husband, and extraordinary coach". I drafted answers to all of the questions above, but my heart and soul came back to these three critical roles, and wanting to be at my very best for each of them. These three roles especially answered the question, "Why do I exist?". I could not think of any better reason to exist than to be an exceptional version of myself for my children, my wife, and my clients. I am not sure why these life roles felt so significant, but at the time of writing this purpose statement, my anchor in life was my family, with my love for my wife and sons keeping me on track and, during some isolated cases, alive. I could not imagine a life without them, nor a scenario in which they didn't have me in their lives.

Over the course of four or five years, I was drowning in a life dominated by mild to moderate depression and experiencing darker thoughts than I ever thought possible. On the surface, I was high-functioning, holding a six-figure management consulting position for an international firm, leading executive coaching and culture change projects throughout New Zealand and Australia. Underneath, I was just trying to catch the local bus safely, without stumbling over my catastrophic thinking.

My mild depression was an underlying level of permanent sadness, with very low expectations for any level of joy or satisfaction on a day-to-day basis. Moderate depression felt like walking through molasses, with every action requiring deliberate and intentional motivation. Life felt like "going through the motions", and being on autopilot was a life-saving strategy. My rare bouts of severe depression led to a dramatic loss of hope for the future and a dangerous feeling that the world would be better off without me.

Many friends and family may read this for the first time with a feeling of shock, wondering how they didn't know. As the person struggling and navigating my own mental health condition, dealing with the situation privately felt like the right thing to do at the time. I am writing this in part to inform those who come after me, who might also be afflicted/blessed with a mental health condition, that there is no right way to deal with it, finding the strength internally to persevere and never give up, or by reaching out for help, as the 'R U OK?' movement would advocate.

The scary part about mental health is the ease with which you fall into the trap of suffering in silence. I felt I had no-one to talk to, and in my state, had no desire to talk to anyone for fear that my crazy and often socially unacceptable thinking would influence the way others thought about me. This held true for extended family, friends, and even my relationship with Fiona and close local friends. I was aware that I was taking my life into my own hands and, as a result, had to develop strategies to keep me safe through a normal day or week. My purpose statement was a tangible lifeline that kept me alive more than once. Feeling deeply connected to my sons and my wife felt like riding an ocean of chaos, clinging to a life raft of hope and love.

While some days were harder than others, I was able to build more and more resilience over time. I navigated those years delicately but successfully in the end, to the point where my belief in my purpose statement became fundamental to who I am. While aspirational at the time that I wrote it, I have grown into the meaning behind the purpose statement and am now on the receiving end of daily feedback (from my children, my wife, and my clients) that reassures me that the statement is true.

HIGHER PURPOSE

Sometimes when we least expect it, an inspiration comes to us that defies logic or seems crazy based on our current circumstance. Sometimes, a chance encounter will change your path forever. For example, my own expectations and aspirations to become a doctor or physiotherapist were happily derailed through an inspiring conversation where I was convinced to pursue an MBA in health services management.

That decision led to a 12-year career in the pharmaceutical industry, full of rich and rewarding experiences including finding an employer who helped facilitate my long-distance relationship with Fiona. Nearly 30 years later, I am in the process of building a strengths-based healthcare programme that combines my knowledge and expertise in the world of healthcare, CliftonStrengths, and business coaching to help cultivate extraordinary health practices in New Zealand. This path could not have been created without the serendipity of that original inspiring conversation.

I see now that my passion for coaching was unlikely to be developed as a health professional, though it would have expressed itself in other ways. My route into business, management and organisational effectiveness allowed my skill and love for coaching to become the core of my career and business. I have always felt that this is centre to my purpose, making dreams come true, which plays out in my relationships with family, friends and clients. I have been proud of my ability to listen to my heart as well as my head in making key decisions influencing my life. My most important decisions were very much dominated by my heart.

Which decision(s) would benefit from more heart and less head?

How did you make some of your best decisions in life?

What role did serendipity play in some of the key decisions of your life?

PURPOSE REVISITED

Nearly ten years after my initial mental health crisis, and approximately six years after writing my original purpose statement, I attended a communications masterclass with Paul Scanlon in Auckland. During his session, he challenged the participants with a new purpose question that I have fallen in love with, given its capacity to unlock people's potential:

"What problem are you here to solve, that only you are uniquely poised to solve?".

We are all uniquely wired to be, do, or create something… what is it for you? There are billions of problems in the world right now, some big, some small – which problem is uniquely yours to solve? This could be isolated to your immediate family, community, or workplace, or it could be grander, focusing on global or universal challenges.

For me, connecting this philosophical question to my life roles of being a great dad, loving husband, and extraordinary coach, I realised that I am here to make dreams come true. These are the problems or challenges that I am uniquely poised to solve, in order of priority: my own dreams, those of my family, my clients, and my community. Other people would scarcely believe in my purpose if I was not able to make my own dreams come true AND have enough spare energy and inspiration to help other people's dreams come true as well.

Inspiring and pursuing a Greatest Imaginable Challenge for myself and the people around me is one way that I have invested in helping make dreams come true. In Chapter 8, we will explore the art of crafting a Greatest Imaginable Challenge from the foundations of what you are most passionate about, what you do best in life or work, and where you can add the most value to yourself or others.

For more information about developing or creating your own purpose statement, have a look at the following resource.

https://christophermiller.co.nz/wp-content/uploads/purpose-creator-for-individuals.pdf

> *Be brave enough to live the life of your dreams according to your vision and **purpose** instead of the expectations and opinions of others.*
>
> — Roy T Bennett, The Light in the Heart

CHAPTER 3

Discovering and Living Your Unique Values

Values are like fingerprints. Nobody's are the same,
but you leave 'em all over everything you do.

Elvis Presley

V ALUES FELT VERY intangible to me for the first 40 years of my life, though they guided my decisions more than I realised at the time. Whether you have reflected on or articulated your values in a formal way or not, they travel with you wherever you go and are made transparent through the choices you make and the preferences you show along the way. The more able you are to articulate them, the more you can use them consciously, to make decisions and take actions towards FISH.

What do you care most about in work and life?

_____

_____

_____

_____

Few questions unearth an individual's core values more clearly than this one. It's interesting to explore what you *say* you care about most versus what behaviours you exhibit that *validate* how much you care about that value.

For example, many people will *say* that family or love are near the top of their list of values, and yet they spend 60 hours a week away from their families, in a job they do not love. When behaviours are in conflict with what we say is important to us, it often causes internal conflict and stress that can only be relieved if we change our value or take a different action.

Which of your own values are conflicted at the moment? What can you do to resolve this?

Value statements have become common in workplaces around the world, but often these are either inappropriately aspirational, or the product of a few sheltered leaders in the organisation, who are out of touch with the most inspirational or destructive behaviours on display. Moreover, leaders and managers are often ill-equipped to have meaningful purpose and values conversations with their team members, who need to focus on their lives, and not just their contribution at work. This often explains why many organisations seem to pay lip service to their core values, given that leaders may treat these behavioural norms as appropriate for their followers, but see them more as loose guidelines for themselves. This is the fastest way to destroy a company culture, and often the reason high performers leave an organisation.

MEANINGFUL VERSUS MEANINGLESS CORE VALUES

My own career journey, from the pharmaceutical and biotech industries in the UK to management consulting and business coaching in New Zealand and Asia-Pacific, is deeply informed by alignment and mis-alignment of values through a variety of employers.

Schering Health Care (now part of the Bayer Group) was a compelling organisation to work for. It held my interest for over five years. Visionary and compassionate leadership, coupled with truly meaningful contributions to health, were informed by a sense of inclusion and purpose (at least for me) that was difficult to ignore or deny. My manager for most of those years, Sue Adams, had an exceptional ability to help me feel supported whilst granting me the freedom and independence to execute substantial company projects that felt essential and critical at the time. For example, launching the UK's first over-the-counter emergency contraceptive and a new insertion technique for the Mirena intra-uterine system. In retrospect, Sue brought out the best in me by living her values transparently and expecting me to do the same, while aligning our common purpose to help progress the company's objectives. Senior leaders of the company had created the same 'we trust you' atmosphere, while engaging in complex problem solving or accessing new resources when and where necessary.

One of the tests of my loyalty to Schering Health Care, which is located in Southeast England, and their loyalty to me, came when I met my Scottish partner, who could not and would not move to England given the need for her to requalify in law. For nearly four years, I held increasingly responsible roles within the company while routinely commuting from Scotland to Southeast England, both through our engagement and for the first year and a half of our marriage. At the time, my commitment to career achievements was as high or higher than my commitment to love and family, but this slowly changed over my years at the company, influenced by more quality time with Fiona.

Eventually, my value of wanting to build a life and a family with Fiona overcame my willingness to experience the inconvenience of such a long-distance commute, despite the terrific employment atmosphere that Schering Health Care had created.

Core values have the potential to push you away, or repel you, as well as pull you forward.

When have you been positively influenced by the values of an organisation you have belonged to?

My next career adventure involved an American biotech company whose European headquarters were located in Glasgow. As a family, this suited us very well and gave us the courage to invest in our first home together, as well as plan for our first child.

The job gave me the opportunity to manage others for the first time, and I led marketing teams ranging from two to seven staff. I took pride in emulating my previous boss at Schering Health Care in building an empathetic approach toward my team members, and desperately – sometimes too desperately – wanting to see them thrive in their roles and in life outside of work. This philosophy did not sit nearly as well in an aggressive, bottom-line focused firm that viewed staff as resources to be moved around and expended at will.

This clash in values came to a head when the company went into a rapid restructure, and with very little consultation or notice period, three members of my team were made redundant (after nearly no consultation with me, their manager). My feeling of powerlessness throughout the process, and not understanding the business justification for the redundancies, led me to one of my first mental health breakdowns, wherein I believe my own reaction to the situation was far greater than those in my team who had been made redundant. To its credit, the company's support systems during my breakdown were timely and effective, but my opinion about the company was damaged from that point forward, and it was not long before the misfitting values led me to seek employment elsewhere.

Interestingly, I still have fond memories of my team and many of the leaders in the company who had good intentions and congruent values. However, a handful of individuals in powerful positions were able to make consistently anti-values-based decisions, all in anticipation of a better bottom line, with little regard to the wake of their hurricane. I suspect these decisions were consistent with the values of those leaders, I am just not sure they were shared by the majority of employees at the time.

When have you noticed a misalignment in core values at a place of work? How was this resolved for you?

LIVING CORE VALUES

Upon arriving in New Zealand, I had the opportunity to join a business coaching company with national reach, whose formula for business success was based on much of the best literature in this field from around the world. The principles of building companies with a foundation of clear purpose and values were fundamental to the coaching services we provided, and I was proud to impact a variety of small businesses in Wellington.

The firm had its own clear set of values, many of which I agreed wholeheartedly with and were very much congruent with my own personal values. Even though we taught values creation to our clients, the company was far from perfect in its own implementation. A couple of examples stood out for me, such as:

* "People first" was one of the firm's values. However, when the values were published, this particular value was ranked fourth in the overall list of values – perhaps a subtle reminder that three other values were more important than people.

* "Live what we teach" was also one of the firm's values – as a business coaching company, I felt it a relevant question to ask the owner at the time who his own business coach was. Surprisingly, there was no immediate answer, which felt very uncomfortable for us both.

I highlight these examples to demonstrate that even when you live in the spirit of values creation and living your values every day, the opportunity for incongruence exists all the time. These inconsistencies are not meant to be held over everyone's head as mistakes, but rather as course corrections to discover how to simplify and breathe life into a set of values every single day.

When have you found it easy to live your organisation's core values? When was it difficult?

BUILDING CORE VALUES

The missing link in most corporate or small business purpose and values setting processes is the implicit and explicit link to everyone's personal core purpose and values. From the CEO to the cleaner, every single person has an essential purpose *and* contributes to the core values of the organisation by expressing their own personal values every day. Just because certain organisation values are written on the wall does not mean anyone is living them consistently. In many cases, organisation values are written in direct conflict to the personal values of some or many staff members.

I used to help companies build values from the perspective of: "What's most important to us in this business?". Over many years, I have realised that it is more powerful to begin with: "What's most important to us as people?" Then, as a business. How do we intend to treat one another? How do we intend to treat our customers, suppliers, and strategic partners? How is this reflected in how we would like to be treated ourselves?

While many values tend to be aspirational, I encourage clients to ground at least 50% of their values in current reality. What can we say is true today? What are the best aspects of working here? What are we most proud of? Only then should we ask what we would like to become. What value would we aspire to have in five years, and why would it serve us differently to our core values today?

MY PERSONAL VALUES

Through experimentation of process and content, I have evolved my own personal and business values over time. My initial personal values list began during a period of extreme journaling as I recovered from the mental health episode outlined in the first chapter.

Through this process, I kept asking:

* What is most important to me right now?
* How do I know what is more important from a list of 'Most important things'?
* How do I rank my values into a list that will help me make rational future decisions?

From these questions came the following list of personal values:

1) Family
2) Health and well-being
3) Life is fun and easy
4) Honour the evolution
5) Live life out loud
6) Creative and financial freedom
7) Thirst for knowledge
8) Hunger for experience.

Family drives nearly every decision I make, and the freedom of working for myself gives me the ultimate flexibility to be with my immediate family any time they need me. Given the health crisis we currently find ourselves in, I wouldn't have it any other way. While the emotional energy of family sits primarily with my wife and two boys here in New Zealand, my role as a son, son-in-law, brother, uncle, nephew, great nephew, etc. play a significant part in how connected I feel to wider whānau. My value of 'family' brings me love and belonging, without fail.

My definition of **health and well-being** used to be quite narrow (physical health) but has expanded over time into mental, emotional, and spiritual health, and now includes my sense of purpose as well as social, community, and financial aspects of well-being (derived from *Well-Being* by Tom Rath and Jim Harter). It has led me to explore mindfulness, local volunteering for diving, and mental health strategies far more fully than had I not prioritised this value.

Funnily enough, the third in the list, **life is fun and easy**, did not exist in my original list, but rather came as a realisation that my wife and eldest son lived that value so completely that I could not help but adopt it as one of my own, even though my natural tendency is to make things intense (at times) and over-complicated! This value has helped me to uncomplicate my life and enjoy the journey with a lot more freedom of thought and emotion. It also helps me feel more connected to my family, who live this value with ease and grace.

Honour the evolution has stemmed from my time as a personal and business development coach. It helps me respect the pace of my own development, and that of my clients. Just because something can be done quickly, doesn't mean it has to be done that way. We also may need to respect the fact that additional time at one level may save us time and effort at a future higher level.

Living life out loud gets easier over time, especially as those close to me understand its intent. It's about having the confidence to speak your truth, even in the face of negativity or objection. Many of the personal revelations in this book are direct results of this value. Part of it is role modelling, both successes and failures, but also engaging with the world and not being a silent observer, which unfortunately is how most people treat social media these days.

I grappled with **freedom** as a value until I realised that, more specifically, I am aspiring to have creative and financial freedom throughout the rest of my life. This value was the catalyst for my departure from management consulting and sponsored executive coaching. It led me to setting up on my own business, and therefore being able to craft and promote my own ideas and intellectual property rather than sell someone else's.

Thirst for knowledge stems directly from my CliftonStrengths pattern, which includes the characteristic of Learner at #2. In CliftonStrengths language, a learner is characterised by having a great desire to learn and to continuously improve. I love absorbing new concepts and feeling inspired by individuals who have something new and interesting to say. Virtual conferences have replaced face-to-face events as my favourite place to learn, but I am hopeful that opportunities to congregate will return post-pandemic. Given my wife's Learner at #1, we are constantly on the lookout for new experiences and sources of inspiration.

Hunger for experience is the natural extension of thirst for knowledge. Once learned, a new concept, idea, or thought has the potential to be experienced. This value theme has propelled me to move continents twice and change careers even more than that.

These values are framed in order of priority for me most of the time. As a result of the order, it becomes easy to make decisions –giving up a great job for a life with my wife, for example – and my inner compass is rarely conflicted. During moments of indecision, my list of values is an easy reference point that helps me to identify a way forward. As time passes, I often reflect on amending or improving on these values. These changes are mostly informed by my desire to develop shared values with the people I care about most.

Based on your intuition, what do you believe are your top three personal core values right now?

EXAMPLES OF CLIENT VALUES

More recently, my clients and I have developed a more circular version of a value set, like the face of a clock. Each value has potentially equal weight, but they can all be used in any moment, and in combination, to help drive a decision or an action.

On the following pages are two examples of recent clients' value sets.

Family: *To love and be surrounded by love as the most powerful force in the universe.*

Surfing: *Experiencing the stoke and bliss that provides my mind and body with relaxation, wellness, peace and freedom to be the best human being I can.*

Openness *is the foundation of my strength to connect with and live a life that is true to me.*

Freedom and flexibility *to pivot life and business around things that are most important.*

Affluent lifestyle *provides me with the ability to prioritise family experiences, freedom, flexibility and the giving of financial support.*

Giving of support: *Whether emotional or financial, the delight in supporting my family, my clients and my community.*

Ease: *Not that things are 'easy' but are done from a state of ease.*

Flexibility: *To generate my own income by working smarter and more efficiently that allows me to pivot between business and personal at anytime.*

Openess: *To show up with an open heart, and be transparent in my communication at all times.*

Support: *To ensure my clients see what's possible and find the confidence in themselves to be bigger and better at what they do.*

Ease: *To approach tasks from a mindset of ease, and where things are not aligned with my strengths and core values to let them go.*

Creativity: *Flexing my creative muscles to enjoy what I do, while finding better ways to show up and connect with my community and clients.*

Action: *To always be taking strategic action towards my goals. Action provides clarity, imperfect action is better than no action.*

One of the essential elements of coaching values, whether personal or business, is the importance of suspending judgement at all times. There are very few situations where a value set could be deemed "wrong". They are always *right* for that individual, and their purpose is to serve them in making better decisions and living life well. Conflict happens when two people have clashing value sets, or when someone is in denial of their own value set. But neither of these problems mean the value set itself is wrong.

Helping a client understand how sets of values might conflict with one another or lead to conflict with the important people in their lives is a useful journey of exploration. This can be done through observation and reflective questioning. Guiding them to let go of self-judgement on their own value set may free them up to live true to their values, rather than pretending that they match with the societal values they see around them.

PRACTICE VALUES

The value set I developed for my coaching and mentoring practice came soon after the development of my personal values. Essentially, this brought a workplace lens to my core and aspirational values. It was also created in a way that was highly congruent with my personal values.

My practice values can be described as follows:

* Do what I love and love what I do (inspired by strengths philosophy).
* Live my why and help others find theirs (inspired by Simon Sinek).

* Every week is a seven-day weekend (inspired by Ricardo Semler).
* Work when inspired, the rest of the time, play!
* Transparency and confidentiality, balanced and fairly applied.

My personal purpose and value themes – make dreams come true, life is fun and easy, live life out loud, and creative and financial freedom – feel highly congruent with the list above. This ensures that I can live my personal and professional values simultaneously with ease.

How are your personal and workplace values congruent? When might they be in conflict?

DEVELOPING YOUR OWN PERSONAL VALUE SET:

1) The following questions may have several different answers. Write them all down on separate Post-it Notes.
   a. What do I care about most in my life right now?
   b. What do I care about most at work right now?
2) Now you have a collection of value statements, select one to compare with each of the others, asking yourself:
   a. Which value is more important to me in life right now?
      i. Hold onto the value that you rate *most important*

throughout the exercise, and place this at the top of your list.

ii. Choose another value and compare it to the rest of the value statements in a similar manner. Repeat this process until you have sorted them all into an ordered list.

3) Review your list and consider how you might make each value statement uniquely yours or offer your own personal definition of what the value means to you. For example, 'love' and 'family' often appear in people's value lists, but the definition or scope of these values is often personal to the individual. Equally, the unique nature of a few of my own values, including 'honour the evolution', developed over time in the context of my chosen profession.

You will notice that the question asks what you care about in life **right now.** While you can take a retrospective view, I have found that deciding on your value preferences in the moment based on your intuition is an effective way to identify and prioritise your series of value statements.

Our values are a powerful force for directing our lives in a positive direction. Very rarely have I ever seen someone invest in the process of creating or discovering their values, only to have chosen themes or intentions that were negative for themselves or others.

Offering the most inspiration are individuals (current and historical) who seem to epitomise a value for humanity, just by the public decisions they have made and the example they have set. For me, examples of this include Mahatma Gandhi (peace),

Princess Diana (compassion), and Nelson Mandela (justice and freedom). None of these individuals were perfect, nor did they ever claim to be, but they had phenomenal discipline and consistently lived their values, even in the face of extraordinary hardship, persecution, or public attention. We make the world a better place when we embody our values.

> *Be the change you wish to see in the world.*
>
> — Mahatma Gandhi

> *Carry out a random act of kindness, with no expectation of reward, safe in the knowledge that one day someone might do the same for you.*
>
> — Diana Spencer

> *As I walked out the door toward the gate that would lead to my freedom, I knew if I didn't leave my bitterness and hatred behind, I'd still be in prison.*
>
> — Nelson Mandela

CHAPTER 4

Understanding FISH

One fish
Two fish
Red fish
Blue fish.

Dr Seuss

W ITH AN UNDERSTANDING of our purpose and our values – and the fact that they are fluid and grow with us throughout life – we can now set out on the journey of finding FISH. This is not an arduous task, nor something you can get right or wrong. This is something to bring you joy. As we move through this chapter, we'll learn how to score your FISH and how to order them. At different times, different parts of FISH will have different priorities for you, and this is completely normal. Fulfilment, inspiration, success, and happiness are all very personal, which is why you must understand your purpose, your values, what inspires you, how you experience and measure success, and what makes you happy in any given moment. While this is a tall task, the following definitions might help clarify each element.

* The textbook definition of fulfilment:
  1. The achievement of something desired, promised, or predicted.
  2. The meeting of a requirement, condition, or need.
* *The FISH definition of fulfilment: The experience of living your purpose every single day.*

* The textbook definition of inspiration:
  1. The process of being mentally stimulated to do or feel something, especially to do something creative.
  2. A sudden brilliant or timely idea.
  3. The drawing in of breath; inhalation.
* *The FISH definition of inspiration: The spontaneous*

process of thinking, being, creating, or doing something new and creative.

🍁 The textbook definition of success:
 1. The accomplishment of an aim or purpose.
 2. The good or bad outcome of an undertaking.

🍁 *The FISH definition of success: The accomplishment of a desirable outcome or experience.*

🍁 The textbook definition of happiness:
 1. The state of being happy – feeling or showing pleasure or contentment.

🍁 *The FISH definition of happiness: Feeling pleasure or being grateful for someone or something.*

While these definitions seem somewhat arbitrary, they are valuable in determining how to assess and calculate your FISH score based on the following questions:

On a scale of 1 to 10, how much fulfilment did you experience today?

1   2   3   4   5   6   7   8   9   10

How did you live your purpose today?

_____

_____

On a scale of 1 to 10, how much inspiration did you feel today?

1   2   3   4   5   6   7   8   9   10

What were you inspired to think, create, do, or be today?

_____

_____

_____

On a scale of 1 to 10, how successful did you feel today?

1   2   3   4   5   6   7   8   9   10

What were your most outstanding achievements today?

_____

_____

_____

On a scale of 1 to 10, how happy did you feel today?

1   2   3   4   5   6   7   8   9   10

What were you most grateful for today? What brought you pleasure?

_____

_____

_____

Your FISH score is generally a *moment in time*, and the questions above are framed in the context of your most recent day. There is value in tracking these questions in a journal, diary, or in The Joy of Finding FISH app so that you can see your scores over extended periods. Alternatively, you can substitute the word "today" in the questions above with "this week", "month", or "year". Your answers to the open-ended questions will be especially insightful, as they begin to build a picture of what activities, moments, and experiences contribute to your feelings of fulfilment, inspiration, success, and happiness.

My simple rule is: if an activity brings you a desirable feeling (FISH experience), do it repeatedly unless and until the frequency ruins the feeling.

What is your FISH score right now? When was the last time you scored a 10 on any of the FISH items?

DAYS AT THE EXTREME

The way we score our FISH will vary immensely from person to person. Days at the extreme, such as 10:10:10:10 or 0:0:0:0 days, may be rare or frequent depending on mindset. Optimists who see the glass full all the time may see every day as 10:10:10:10 until a challenging day knocks the score down. In contrast, pessimists may regularly give scores below 5, until an exceptionally positive day comes along to push the scores up. Neither is right or wrong, they are just different. This is why it is unhelpful to compare your FISH scores with others'.

Incredibly, a day that *seems* bad may still have a FISH score with one or two high scoring areas. You may not have felt happy, but you may have been fulfilled or inspired. That is the enduring strength of FISH – that it is not based around some simplistic measure of only how we feel, rather it exists on a deeper and future-focused level. Even the simplest, most peaceful of days can score 8:8:8:8, thanks to conscious awareness and gratitude for everyday experiences.

My own worst days have been characterised by my depression; a paralysis that leads to inaction and a pervasive feeling of self-pity. On such days, I feel unable to fulfil my life roles adequately. At these moments, being able to look at the four categories of FISH individually has helped me to find one area that I can focus on, to lift my score up and build momentum again.

THE ORDER OF FISH

The process of finding and creating FISH is more of an art than a science and can change dramatically over time. In particular, our experience of FISH may change through various life stages or personal circumstances. For example, our wild teenage and young adult years may express FISH in a particular order or with a specific flavour. In contrast, later years as a parent or even grandparent may shift both the order and how we experience FISH. This may explain differences in perspective or conflicts between generations, which I will expand on later in the chapter.

Based on the permutations of FISH, 24 sequences can be used to explain the order in which individuals pursue fulfilment, inspiration, success, and happiness. Importantly, there is no incorrect order. Every order is correct for its time and place. Understandably, I chose the order of FISH for the purposes of writing this book, as it was the most evocative! Your letters needn't spell a word for them to have meaning for you.

* FISH, FIHS, FSIH, FSHI, FHIS, FHSI
* IFSH, IFHS, ISFH, ISHF, IHSF, IHFS
* SFIH, SFHI, SIFH, SIHF, SHFI, SHIF
* HFSI, HFIS, HIFS, HISF, HSIF, HSFI

If you had to choose right now, which order would you put the letters in?

MY ORDER OF FISH

The experience and expression of FISH changes depending on circumstances and life stages. For example, during my younger years of academics, sport, and the early stages of my business career, I led with the pursuit of success. I often derived happiness, inspiration, and fulfilment from that success. The understanding I had of my purpose and how to experience fulfilment was so lacking that I am confident my FISH pattern looked more like SIH or SHI, with little or no fulfilment at all. My experience of inspiration and happiness came through my pursuit and achievement of success, rather than the other way around. I also derived great satisfaction from meeting or exceeding my own and other people's expectations of what I was capable of. Rarely did I do things "just because"; my actions were nearly always in search of higher achievement, accolades, or rewards.

Fast forward 20 years, and my pattern of FISH has changed. My mental health crisis, soul searching, and connection to my sense of purpose has moved fulfilment to become my lead FISH element, closely followed by happiness, inspiration and success

(FHIS). All four remain important to me, but the order in which I seek each out has changed over time. My many years of leading with success were a testing ground, from which I am now able to derive a great deal of self-assurance, knowing that when I am centred within my purpose, success (and happiness/inspiration) flows easily.

From Chapter 2, you will recall that my purpose is to make dreams come true – first my own, then my family's, my clients', and my community's. Through the process of delivering on this purpose, I experience happiness (pleasure from the process, gratitude to have the privilege of fulfilling this purpose), inspiration (to see new possibilities for myself and those I help facilitate), and success (to earn the rewards, financial and non-financial, from pursuing these dreams). Fulfilling my purpose and my life roles (be a great dad, a loving husband, and an extraordinary coach), takes priority over happiness, inspiration, and success. It is my foundation from which all the other experiences can be derived.

Today, FHIS is my normal pattern of experiencing FISH, but the process is very fluid and there are moments of pure happiness, inspiration, and success that can and do occur separately from fulfilment. There are no hard and fast rules as to how and why we derive different emotions at different times. For example, the experience of extraordinary moments in nature – beautiful sunrises, or when a monarch butterfly lands within inches of where you are sitting – can create a profound sense of happiness or even inspiration when you least expect it.

Though success has moved from the first position to the last in my current FHIS sequence, it remains an integral part of my life, both personally and professionally. The growth milestones of my coaching practice have all been celebrated in various fashions, contributing even further to happiness along the way.

How does your current order of FISH compare to what it would have been 10 years ago?

FISH ORDER ACROSS GENERATIONS

Based on observations of clients and family, I believe everyone's FISH priorities and subsequent scores fluctuate over time. This may also explain some of the tension that occurs between generations. For example, the mindset of a person who grew up in the 1960's may be dominated by pursuit of happiness and inspiration. For many boomers, this pursuit quickly transformed into a "responsible" success mindset, since their generation is the last to have experienced lifetime careers with employers, traditionally climbing the corporate or public service ladder, retiring with reliable financial security and returning to the pursuit of happiness in retirement.

In contrast, millennials (and the generations that have come since them) find a profound sense of fulfilment and purpose at a very early stage of life and career. This can be misunderstood by older generations who are often the younger generations' leaders or otherwise above them in society. Passion for protesting and doing whatever it takes (think Greta Thunberg), even to the detriment of personal success and reputation, is incredible to watch. Still, these motivations are foreign to a generation that prioritised happiness in younger years, and success through their most productive working years.

Older generations can sometimes forget about the rule-breaking they may have done in their youth and sit in judgement of current younger generations. It would be rare for the order of FISH to be precisely the same, or expressed in the same way, between two individuals of different generations.

What other conflicts do you see in society that might be explained by a different ordering of FISH?

_____

_____

_____

COURAGE TO FOLLOW YOUR PATH

Over more than a decade of business and personal development coaching, I have often been struck by the differences between small business/practice ownership and entrepreneurship, and those who have chosen a career and those who have fallen into one. The FISH order for the group who have chosen to work for themselves is very different from that of the group who have chosen a professional career based on working for someone else.

Somewhere along the way, an entrepreneur or small business leader has been struck by inspiration, usually rooted in one or more aspects of their purpose in life and business.

In contrast, a professional very early in their career (often as early as high school or university) is driven by the rhythm of building success and deriving happiness from each new career milestone.

Neither option is right or wrong; they are simply motivated by different emotions or experiences, that get reinforced by family, friends, and peers. Thus, a habit of IFHS (entrepreneur) or SHFI (career professional) is created for each.

CHALLENGES OF BEING A CAREER PROFESSIONAL

One of the sad consequences of societal or parental expectations, and the actual or perceived status and earning potential
that comes with certain career choices (following medicine or
law, for example) is the creation of whole generations of trapped
professionals. These individuals have creative aspirations beyond
their professions but are unable to extricate themselves from
many years of sunk costs in terms of education, training, and
the routine of maintaining their professional standing in society.
It is a brave lawyer or doctor who re-frames their life at the age
of 40 or 50 in order to pursue what their heart truly desires. It is
no coincidence that mental health challenges are becoming more
prominent across these groups.

Effective strategies for overcoming feelings of being trapped
in a professional role include:

* Taking an extended break from the profession – or
  having one forced on you with a breakdown!
* Reconnecting with purpose and the reasons why you
  have more to contribute (considering your future legacy
  in particular).
* Identifying ways to give back to the community or the
  world, either in a related field or a completely different
  and unique way.
* Re-branding and creating a new identity by investing
  in thought leadership that moves beyond the norms of
  the profession.
* Building interests/ hobbies/ communities that have
  nothing to do with the chosen profession.

* Resetting values and making lifestyle changes that reduce dependency on the reputation and financial income of the profession.

Having the courage to follow your path requires a detachment from the expectations placed upon you often by those who care about you most. You might have a partner, children, parents, or friends who have only known you as one thing (professionally), and they may have never been exposed to the hopes and dreams that are in direct conflict with their own well-being, especially when financial.

CHALLENGES OF BEING AN ENTREPRENEUR

There is a downside and trap for the entrepreneur who leads with inspiration and fulfilment… and may never bring an idea to fruition. Constantly inspired by new ideas, they might be accused of "magpie syndrome", flitting from one shiny object to another, never entirely completing any one potential vision of the future. While some entrepreneurs have a built-in sense of success strong enough to propel an idea from conception to fulfilment, often serial entrepreneurs require partnerships with others to build the success they are capable of.

Below are some ideas to help with building achievement as an entrepreneur.

* Make an honest assessment of the gaps in your skillset. Build a team around you that balances out these gaps.
* Practise sitting in a moment and finding happiness in the

small things, as an alternative to leaping from one idea to the next.

* Maintain your attraction to shiny new things, but dial the perspective inwards, so that you're searching for shiny new ways to build and improve your current ideas.
* Take the time to define what success looks like for you. It's fine if it doesn't fit into society's ideal of success. Nonetheless, be clear on what it is for you.

How do you feel about your current profession or dominant pastimes? What aspects are most fulfilling for you? Do you lean towards inspiration or success at the moment?

_____

_____

_____

_____

If you could get paid to do what you love, what would you do?

_____

_____

_____

MOMENTS OF DECISION AND DESTINY

When considering our FISH order, we are often confronted by an intuitive response so strong that it is difficult to deny the impulse to make a dramatically courageous decision, even in the face of adversity or objections from those we love most. Two moments like this stand out to me when I look back on the last 50 years of my life. The first occurred in the penultimate year of my four-year undergrad degree in Life Sciences at Queen's University in Kingston, Ontario. Having followed a fairly traditional pre-med degree in Canada, I had always assumed that I would extend my love of health sciences to complete a medical or physiotherapy degree, both of which were offered to a high standard at Queen's.

Whilst I was considering my decision, I met an extraordinary individual who was full of positivity, energy, and vitality. At the end of her degree, she had previously left Queen's to pursue an MBA in Health Services Management at McMaster University in Hamilton, Ontario. The business of healthcare had never really entered my radar at the time, but the passion and persuasive arguments that this person offered about the programme at McMaster were overwhelmingly convincing, including the fact that it was a co-operative degree over two and a half years, combining academic terms with sponsored work terms in a health care setting. The latter appealed as it would build a solid resume of relevant experience before I set out into the "real world".

I was inspired to apply to McMaster and was accepted into their MBA Health Services Management programme in September 1993. Over the next couple of years, I came to deeply understand and appreciate the complexities of both private (e.g., pharmaceuticals and medical diagnostics) and public (teaching hospital management) health care sectors. These learnings included the subtle way health care services are marketed and sold in the Canadian marketplace which set me up for success later in the European pharmaceutical industry. One of my proudest moments was being nominated as valedictorian of my graduating class in December 1995. My journey from potential health practitioner to health care business advisor, marketer, and business builder was complete.

A second destiny moment occurred when my family and I emigrated from Scotland to New Zealand in 2007. Following a 12-year career in pharmaceutical and biotech marketing, I had the opportunity to reinvent myself into the New Zealand marketplace. During a going-away event in a café in Glasgow, a friend of ours had a toddler playing with a two-sided rattle. As a bit of a laugh, we placed bets on which side the rattle would fall each time the toddler dropped it. As the stakes grew higher, I said, "Heads – I stay in pharmaceuticals, and we move to Auckland; tails – I build a career as a business coach, and we head for Wellington".

The rattle came up tails and the rest is history… I have built a 14-year career in business and executive coaching and management consulting, based in the best little capital city I can think of. The lifestyle and opportunities that this choice brought me have been immense. Re-entering the pharmaceutical industry in New Zealand would have led to frustration at the same-ness of it all. My career as a business coach has brought huge variety and exceptionally positive and challenging experiences – all thanks to the flip of a rattle!

One handy decision-making tool that is shared in many forums is the coin-flip technique. When faced with two equally compelling options, flip a coin to choose between them. The power of this process is not in which side the coin falls, but which option you most hope is chosen while the coin is in the air. Alternatively, which option would you be most disappointed in when the coin flip is revealed? In every moment, we have the power to choose, even when we pretend to let fate decide.

THE PATH OF LEAST RESISTANCE

I often hear people say, "Just lean in and get it done!", but I am never convinced by this advice. My younger self would have taken it and applied it wholeheartedly. I often committed to long hours, avoiding asking for assistance because I felt the whole solution or project had to come from me.

Twenty years of pain later, I am a big advocate of the question: "Who can do it better than me?" – there is always someone. It is now clear to me that other individuals with different strengths and different FISH orders will tackle problems from fresh angles, and our combined approach will inevitably be stronger than either of us acting individually.

For example, someone who leads with happiness will inject fun and light-heartedness, resulting in everyone valuing the journey as well as the result. Someone leading with success will often "lean in and get it done" at just the right time for the project, while an individual leading with inspiration will look for new ways of thinking or doing that the rest of the team wouldn't have thought of. Finally, someone who leads with fulfilment will look for the profound reason behind the project and how it affects more comprehensive systems, and they will help align the purpose of everyone in the team to achieve a common objective.

The path of least resistance offers a strategy to lean into what you do best, and what you find easiest to perform at your highest level, **while allowing everyone around you to do the same!** Perhaps the exception is a learning challenge where you have not yet, but wish to, improve a skill or process that you have not done frequently enough to master. Even in these situations, a coach or mentor is ideally positioned to help you fast-track the learning. It is their role to guide you expertly along the way.

HEART VERSUS HEAD

It's often said that human beings have at least three brains – our head, our heart, and our gut. Many advocate for one over the others based on their personal preference or what has worked for them in the past. More commonly, it is thought useful to understand how to use these three sources of decision making in tandem, allowing the relevant one forward at the right time, depending on the context of the decision.

Our head might be relied on to sift through vast amounts of information or data, and to evaluate our past experiences (memory) to decide what the best action to take next might be. The heart-brain would be prominent in an emotional decision, where strong feelings are at play and may influence the outcome. Finally, the gut-brain (or intuition) would help us navigate desirable outcomes, especially when confronted with limited data or information to back up the decision. This last might be a source of momentum towards a destiny, even if this destiny is not fully known or articulated.

The brain in our head has also been postulated to have three different regions – the primal brain, the emotional brain, and the rational brain (*Triune Brain* – Paul MacLean). These have parallels with the gut (primal), heart (emotional), and head (rational) brains described previously. Given the complexity of human biology and how much we have yet to understand, exceptional decision making may lie at the junction of all of these brains and our ability to identify which brain should take precedence in any given situation.

ANY DECISION IS THE RIGHT DECISION (VERSUS NO DECISION)

Whether looking at your fulfilment/purpose, your inspiration/ ideas, your success/achievements, or your happiness/contentment, each step in your pursuit of FISH deserves a decision. This decision will usually come *after* a period of expansion where you might explore every possibility that might bring you FISH. Once you have examined the possibilities, it is important to *choose* the option(s) that has the greatest chance of lifting your fulfilment, inspiration, success, and happiness. It may be the case that, following a period of inspiration and expanded ideas, focusing on choosing a specifically limited option will contribute best to your experience of fulfilment, success, and happiness.

A decision *not* to do something is better than no decision. Many people get trapped in the vortex of procrastination and the downward spiral of indecision. For many, committing to a decision to say no or eliminate an option is significant progress toward what they might want or need. Exceptional individuals in the Thought Leaders (www.thoughtleaders.com.au) community often refer to the root definition of "decide" (to cut or kill off), which shares its core with words like homicide (to kill another), regicide (to kill the king), suicide (to kill oneself), etc. Think of "deciding" in terms of killing off choices and identifying the only option left after all other options are eliminated.

In sporting pursuits such as football, hockey, or ultimate

frisbee, the decision to choose a direction (thus eliminating the other directions) often opens up the possible routes of success. Prior to making that decision, it seemed like you had a wealth of options, but actually the indecision of standing still would most likely have led to failure. The action of movement may create the likelihood of a pass completion, as it prevents the defence from anticipating the direction of play. Equally, you may not be able to tell which is the best direction until you have started moving and gathered more information. Sometimes, the value is in letting go of options in order to decide on a single way forward.

Finding FISH might be better described as choosing FISH – choose wisely!

What is your big idea to change your life for the better, and what is the next action you need to take?

What were your top three achievements in life so far? The next 'top three achievements' are in your future – what are they?

Life is what you make it. Find your own path to fulfilment. — Anonymous

To succeed, you need to find something to hold on to, something to motivate you, something to inspire you. — Tony Dorsett

Happiness is not a goal. It's a by-product of a life well lived. — Eleanor Roosevelt

---

Coming soon: The Joy of Finding FISH App, which will include keeping a diary of your FISH score and unique strategies for lifting fulfilment, inspiration, success and happiness. Scan the QR code below to get an update on when the app will become available.

CHAPTER 5

Integrating Life Roles

It's not time to make a change
Just relax, take it slowly
You're still young, that's your fault
There's so much you have to go through.
Find a girl, settle down
If you want you can marry
Look at me, I am old, but I'm happy.

Father and Son – Cat Stevens

NTEGRATING LIFE ROLES is all about identifying – and creating identity from – all the roles you play. Professional, personal, family, community; all are relevant to thriving as an individual and contributing to the lives of those you care about most. Life roles may also be reflected in your core values, with those most important to you represented in both a life-role map and your expression of values. A life-role map is a visual representation of all of the relationships in your life. It is a useful tool for prioritising where to invest your time and energy. This concept will be explored more later in the chapter.

My previous purpose statement, which served me very well for over six which years, was: "To be a great dad, a loving husband, and an extraordinary coach". Having discovered and evolved my subsequent purpose statement (to make dreams come true), I realised that my former purpose statement still had immense value in my life. These have since become my key life roles, which sit alongside my purpose statement as a source of inspiration and direction.

Over time, it has become clear to me that there are many life roles that I occupy and that the concept of a *life role* adds value, especially toward how I prioritise the relationships in my life. The following figure explores some of my many life roles, with the most important being at the centre of the diagram:

The very process of identifying and mapping your own life roles may be quite illuminating to you, as it reveals just how many significant parts you play in the lives of others. In my case, it began with a positive focus on my roles as a husband and a father, as these are of highest importance to me in everyday life.

*In order of importance, who are the **most** important people in your life right now?*

_____

_____

_____

SELF-CARE FIRST, RELATIONSHIPS SECOND (EVEN THE MOST IMPORTANT ONES)

The first version of my life-role map had husband and father in the very centre of the diagram. Yet, when I reflected on my ability to actually fulfil these roles, it seemed that my investment in self-care was paramount, and had to precede my roles as husband and father. If I am not healthy and do not have enough energy to play my crucial life roles, I cannot fulfil those responsibilities, or may do so inadequately. Hence managing my bipolar condition with medication, exercise, sleep, mindfulness, and moments to myself are all critical to my ability to give back to the relationships that I value most in life. This very much aligns with my #2 value, health and well-being, which was explored in Chapter 3, but I recognise the contradiction this creates given that family is my #1 value. All of these concepts and models can be very fluid, with different elements taking priority at different times.

As you travel toward the exterior of the key life-role map, you may identify more roles are important to you. Friendships, working relationships, and relationships with relatives who may be distant in one way or another will form part of the life-role map, and a role's distance from the centre may indicate how much time, trust, or love is invested in that relationship. In my case, my relationship with my parents, brother and sister, and my coaching/mentoring clients all sit at the next level for various reasons. Though my family are far away, I always feel deeply connected with them and care enormously for their happiness and success. The unconditional support and encouragement that I get from my family in Canada gives me great strength and contributes to my resilience.

Equally important are my coaching and mentoring clients. Most of these relationships exist in New Zealand, but I also have a growing number of critical relationships internationally. I prioritise these individuals as I care deeply about their own achievement of FISH, and my family's financial well-being is partly dependent on the value-exchange implied by these client relationships. I also view my clients' success journeys as evidence of my growing legacy and impact on a group of talented individuals dotted around the world. Even with former clients, I relish stories about their courage and achievements where a seed may have been sown back when we worked together. I am also very aware that in New Zealand, as elsewhere, reputation and results quickly lead to repeat and/or referral opportunities. It is no accident that I treat many of my client relationships with as much care as many of my family relationships.

Around the periphery of my life-role map lie many roles that demand less time or less energy to maintain. These aren't necessarily less important. They capture the many additional relationships that I have been able to easily identify. Some are transactional (taxpayer), while others are platonic or familial. With these relationships, frequency of communication (and therefore connection) may be less intense than the roles closer to the centre of the circle. My hope with these relationships is that I am present and available with as much energy and time as possible and reciprocate the generosity of those individuals whenever I can.

NON-JUDGEMENTAL APPROACH TO LIFE-ROLE MAP

Like the discussions about values, it is essential to recognise that the life-role map is very personal and requires a non-judgemental perspective, even from the person creating it. It may feel challenging to place certain people towards the outer-edge of your map, but this creates opportunity, especially regarding the future investment of time, care, and energy toward that individual.

The life-role map is very fluid, with people moving towards and away from the centre depending on circumstances and your desire to build a stronger relationship with any given individual. It is also not helpful to compare your own life-role map with others, given the personal nature of each and every relationship. One person's deep connection with family members might be another person's ability to connect with close friends or work colleagues. Everyone is different and we all change over time. Our most intimate relationships may shift as we age, and the significance of childhood, parenthood, or grandparenthood will move key people in and out of our inner circles.

It may also be helpful to consider a life-role map that is accurate today, and an aspirational version of the map or what you'd like it to look like in the future. Fostering deeper friendships or higher quality relationships with members of the community you belong to may enhance your FISH experience given the right investment. In a work context, it may be helpful to map out who is in your trusted circle and whom you would like to invest in building more trust. This can be the key to opportunity and success in the workplace.

Your life-role map may also help identify where you spend

the most time, and whether that time is congruent with your personal and professional values. It may be that your immediate family are closest to the centre of your life-role map, but if you are spending 60+ hours a week with people at work, what signal are you sending to your family about where you prefer to spend your time?

Who do you spend the most time with? Who do you speak to most often or with greatest intention?

Who would you value spending more time with right now? How will you orchestrate spending more time with that person?

INTEGRATE AND COMPARTMENTALISE

Most of us are used to the focus of compartmentalising life roles. When I am Dad, I am focused on being with my children and creating meaningful experiences together, or just enjoying each other's company. The most common form of compartmentalising is the switch from home to work that most people do on their commute every day. Covid-19, working from home and flexible working practices are blurring these lines and making it more difficult to compartmentalise work from family.

Integrating life roles is about experiencing multiple functions simultaneously and seamlessly, without sacrificing energy in favour of any one role. The best example of this would be a big family reunion, where you are engaged with multiple generations, a wide range of ages, and quite different individual relationships all at once. Family games, where everyone is having a laugh and celebrating success and failure together, bring memorable moments for everyone and for every life role that each person occupies. Given that my extended family are so far away from each other, these moments are precious, and memories are thankfully captured as photos and videos to re-live for years to come.

What I have noticed over time is the balance between integration and compartmentalisation in the way I invest in my life roles. Sometimes, a single role may require energy and focus (like when I am coaching a client), at other times, there is leverage in fulfilling multiple roles at once. The most obvious example of the latter is when we are spending time as a family, and I am fully invested in my role as a husband and a father simultaneously.

Another great example of integrating life roles for me personally comes in the form of our many family weekends attending springboard and platform diving competitions. Whether at home in Wellington, or elsewhere in New Zealand, these weekends allow me the opportunity to integrate my role as father, husband, diving community member, diving judge, cheerleader, and friend to members of the Wellington Diving Club and/or Diving New Zealand. We all take these types of events for granted, but the way we can simultaneously and seamlessly fulfil so many roles amazes me.

While performing my role as a diving judge for up to (and sometimes more than) an hour, I am 100% focused on the event at hand, ensuring that my attention is on each diver and giving a score that fairly reflects each performance. Only in the event of a dramatic crisis with family members, who are all likely to be nearby, would I extricate myself from the responsibility of judging a diving event. This is perhaps the best example of compartmentalising a role, with singular focus which, in the moment, is very much to the exclusion of all else, while in the context of a weekend spent integrating multiple roles.

My commitment to writing (this book, blogs, newsletters, articles, etc.) is very similar. It requires extended periods of focus, imagination, inspiration, and discipline, and yet most of my writing occurs with my immediate family only a few metres away, fully occupied doing their own thing and intuitively knowing not to interrupt me as I am creating. In a heartbeat, I can shift from writing with purpose to fulfilling my role as a parent by fixing the afternoon snack for the people I love most. None of these interruptions feel difficult or annoying; I know I will find flow again the next time I sit down to write, with the comforting feeling that I have played all of my roles to their fullest that day.

SEAMLESS INTEGRATION – LIFE IS FUN AND EASY

My third value plays a big role in how I integrate key relationships and invest my time with others. If the connection is not already fun and easy, or doesn't have the potential to become so, why am I invested? I often begin to recognise that a friendship or a client relationship may have run its course if it begins to feel too difficult or seems to require a lot of effort to maintain successfully. As Chapter 1 suggests, there are too many brilliant people and wonderful experiences to have in this world to get pulled down by those who seem only to make life difficult.

The spontaneous experience of a magical moment that required no effort whatsoever to create can be impressive. You just had to be present and aware enough to recognise the moment. Personal examples include witnessing my sons experiencing moments of gratitude, and realising that I helped set up their appreciation or the circumstances that led to that moment of gratitude. Hearing my wife sing, because she is happy or inspired in some way, also makes my heart skip a beat, even when it is frequent or to others might seem commonplace (she is on a repetitive loop of *Top of the World* by The Carpenters and *Feeling Good* by Michael Buble).

ADDING A NEW ROLE

Life roles become particularly meaningful when they appear for the very first time. Some we barely notice, like when we are born and become a son or daughter. The significance of becoming a child is lost compared with the profound experience of becoming a parent for the first or subsequent time. The births of our children are moments that are etched into our minds and souls in ways that very few other experiences are comparatively. This remains true whether labour is easy or traumatic, whether the birth occurs as planned or unexpectedly at home!

New roles appear all the time in our lives – starting a new job, starting a business for the first time (or the tenth!), competing in a sporting event, volunteering for a new organisation, or taking on a new responsibility.

New family members may also create new roles such as parent, uncle/aunt, cousin, brother-/sister-in-law, grandparent, etc. Each addition brings new experiences, new perspective, and new relationships to thrive in and contribute to.

A new role, even one as important as parenthood, usually creates a significant moment of uncertainty that is usually expressed as, "Can I do this?". Most parents have moments of doubt prior to having their first child, and yet proceed towards mastery! "Faking it 'til you make it" is an experience nearly everyone navigates at one point in their life. Part of the feeling of success is the ability to work through the fear and uncertainty and come out the other side realising that you CAN do this.

SUBTRACTING A ROLE(S) — CATASTROPHIC CHANGES IN LIFE ROLES

Roles can be added, but they can also be subtracted. Sometimes, this is voluntarily, such as when we resign from a job or step down from a volunteering role. In these cases, it is a matter of *letting go* of the responsibilities of the recent past, often to make space for a new adventure (e.g., changing jobs).

More challenging is the unexpected loss of a role. This might occur through death or divorce. Loss of a parent, spouse, or a child has the potential to have a profound impact on an individual's sense of identity, and the support net that they have created around them. Loss of a loved one prematurely might be defined as catastrophic, challenging every ounce of resilience and strength in the individual(s) affected. The courage required to face loved ones and wider society in the event of the loss of a spouse or child is extreme. Even with a prolonged prognosis, I am not sure anything can quite prepare you for the departure of someone in your immediate family who was engrained in the fabric of everything you experienced.

BUILDING IDENTITY

Each role we occupy also has the power to build or reinforce our personal and professional identity. These roles do not occur in isolation, and our experiences of each have a bearing on, and may bring wisdom to, any of our other roles. Coaching your child's local football team may bring insight to how you manage a team at work. The way you invest in and grow a marriage might inform some of your other most important relationships such as with your best friend, your boss, or a business partner.

Sport in particular offers insight into other facets of life, especially the workplace. Whether training and practising as an athlete, working with teammates, or coaching and encouraging a group of players, roles in sport are highly transferable to work situations where teamwork, collective objectives, and orchestrating talent/resources is the norm.

Critical career decisions and the courage to take on new roles and responsibilities have a defining effect on your sense of self and self-assurance. Significant pivot points for me included:

* Moving from Canada to the U.K. to begin a career in pharmaceuticals,
* Transitioning from home-based/car-based sales to a head office marketing role,
* Managing a team for the first time,
* Moving from Scotland to New Zealand and redefining myself from pharmaceutical marketing executive to business development coach,
* Management consultant to corporate executive coach,
* Employee mindset to entrepreneur's mindset when I started my own business.

Each experience built on the previous one, and I am proud to have occupied so many different roles throughout my career. It is the sum of these experiences that my clients are paying for, along with the business and personal development coach training that I have invested in along the way.

LOVE AND TRUST ACROSS THE ROLES

The life-role map at the beginning of this chapter could be summarised by asking, "Where will I invest the most love and greatest trust across all of my relationships?". The closer to the centre, the more likely you will be to have time, energy, and desire to expand trusting and loving relationships. Remember that the concentric circles and the people who occupy them are moving all the time. In any given moment, any one of your roles can hold precedence and benefit from the intensity of your awareness and attention.

The people at the centre of the life-role map are likely to hold a greater significance in your own experience of FISH, and these individuals in turn will benefit most from your own investment in their FISH! In fact, it is likely that your individual and collective FISH experience with those at the centre of the circle will be so intertwined that the boundaries may get very blurry.

Identifying and defining your key life roles may help prioritise the strongest and most fulfilling relationships in your life. Be prepared for these relationships to ebb and flow as priorities change, but always come back to the question, "Where shall I invest my love and attention today?". In addition, any individual may change their location on the life-role map by unexpectedly investing time in you or by having a meaningful experience with someone that brings them closer to the centre of the circle. Consciously investing time with specific individuals will also change their position on the map.

What roles do you currently play:
- *In your family?*
- *At work?*
- *In your community?*

How might you simplify or integrate these roles to maximise the energy and impact you can contribute?

Earlier, we touched on the idea of mapping aspirational life roles. Doing so may give you an indication as to where you would most like to invest time and energy, and whom you would like to increase time spent with. In particular, lapsed relationships with family or friends have the potential to be rekindled given new shared experiences.

You can use your answers to the questions in this chapter to build an accurate life-role map for yourself today and reflect on an aspirational one if and when specific relationships are improved. The picture of your life-role map will be ever-changing, but is largely in your control when you commit conscious effort to building and maintaining great relationships around you.

> *With every word we utter, with every action we take,*
> *we know our kids are watching us. We as parents are*
> *their most important role models.*
>
> — Michelle Obama

CHAPTER 6

Celebrating Achievement

There's a party goin' on right here
A celebration to last throughout the years
So bring your good times and your laughter too
We're gonna celebrate your party with you!

Celebration - Songwriters: Moses Davis / Luminee
Cedeno / Timofei Crudu / Morlon Greenwood / Efe
Oekmen / Winston Thomas / Calibe Thompson

W E'VE FOCUSED A lot on purpose and on values, which both speak strongly to the FISH measures of fulfilment and inspiration. Now it's time to look at an action linked closely to success, and to moving success from a mere happenstance to something deep and meaningful in your life.

Human beings thrive in creating progress or building a future that is better than their past. Constant and continuous improvement, or even just the simplicity of improving one thing each day, can add tremendous value to a life well lived. Successes and achievements are simply the measuring sticks of these improvements. The greater the achievement, the more significant the progress.

This chapter aims to acknowledge the need and value of celebrating achievement, rather than just moving from one accomplishment to another without reflecting on each significant milestone. The act of stopping to celebrate will often create a platform for the next goals to be built upon. Celebration creates an opportunity to acknowledge the skill, talent, and hard work that led to an achievement, and to derive any learnings along the way that might be relevant for the future. Rushing to the next objective without pausing to celebrate may lead to a lack of insight or learnings to build on. It also renders success fairly meaningless. What is the point of your success if you never stop to appreciate it?

HOW TO TREASURE BOTH CELEBRATION AND ACHIEVEMENT

There is significance in both accomplishing an outcome *and* stopping to celebrate or at least acknowledge the progress made. It is not an either-or. Each achievement will precede a moment of celebration, and that celebration is then tailored to the scale and significance of the accomplishment. Given how many people travel from goal to goal, achievement to achievement, rarely stopping to take stock of their accomplishments, the act of celebration can often be an accomplishment in itself!

One of the most powerful exercises I do for myself and my clients is a 90-day stock-take. We document and reflect on the many achievements over the last three months and draw insights from the challenges that may have occurred along the way.

"We usually overestimate what we think we can accomplish in one year – but we grossly underestimate what we can accomplish in a decade." – Tony Robbins

What were your greatest achievements over the last 90 days?

_____

_____

_____

What were your most outstanding achievements over the last 10 years?

_____

_____

_____

How can you build on those accomplishments in the future?

Once you've reflected on the questions above, consider what achievements deserve a celebration, even in retrospect. Why is a rest or a break valuable in between your past, current, and future achievements? As you set new goals for the future, reflect on how your past achievements set you up for success. Success building is like training at the gym – each repetition and each new weight adds substance and strength to the next or future achievement. This is especially true if you take the time to study what led to your previous successes, and how these can be applied to the future.

In the absence of that stock-take, individuals roll on and on to the next achievements, never realising the progress that is being made. Whether this progress is through learned experience, or accomplishments that contribute to the individual's definition of success and identity, it is important that it is noticed.

More important is the value of a celebration, big or small, to acknowledge accomplishments that have occurred in the recent past. The celebration usually is reflective of the scale of the achievement, and often involves the people we care about most. A new job might warrant a night out for dinner to celebrate, or even bring the prospect of investing in a new house due to a relocation. Sometimes, the celebration is more memorable than the achievement itself, depending on how unique the activity or self-reward is. It is important to emphasise that the achievement and the celebration tend to be separate events or moments in time, and that any time delay between the two is irrelevant if the memory of the achievement is strong and significant. In many cases, small achievements may not demand a celebration, but the cumulative impact of those small achievements does.

Capturing an achievement might be described as acknowledging and savouring the moment of success, identifying a suitable celebration, and then living that celebration experience to the fullest. For me, categories of success include: appreciating a moment of accomplishment, reflecting on a positive experience, acknowledging a life milestone, and witnessing or contributing to another person's success. The following list is of examples in my life for each of those categories.

Appreciating a moment of success:

* Planning and executing the successful launch of the U.K.'s first over-the-counter emergency contraception.
* Being nominated valedictorian for my MBA graduating class.
* Buying my first flat with my wife in Glasgow.

Reflecting on a positive experience:

* Competing for Nova Scotia at the Canada Games as a springboard diver; competing for Queen's University in varsity diving championships (I never won a medal, but the experience was superb!).
* Playing various solos as lead oboist for the Queen's University orchestra.
* Planning and experiencing an unforgettable day in

Queenstown – white water rafting, bungee jump, a vineyard tour and lunch, paragliding, and an evening Mexican meal to celebrate!

Acknowledging a life milestone:

* Engagement to Fiona on the esplanade of Edinburgh Castle during a Texas concert on 31st December 1999.
* Wedding to Fiona in St Giles' Cathedral on 24th February 2001 (it snowed!).
* Births of Cameron and Ross – both caesarean sections, one more stressful than the other.
* Moving continents – from Canada to the U.K. in 1995 and from Scotland to New Zealand in 2007.

Witnessing or contributing to another person's success:

* Fiona cycling from Land's End to John O'Groats in the U.K. – 17 days as support vehicle, banana carrier, and chief cheerleader!
* Fiona completing her PhD over six years on a part-time basis – the pride of reading her final thesis, and the many accolades she has received since for a ground-breaking piece of work, which led to a massive celebration as a family in Dunedin for her graduation weekend in 2019!
* Watching Cameron and Ross learn a new dive and take it into competition, most recently back 2 ½ tuck off 3-metre for Cameron and back 1 ½ tuck off 5-metre for Ross!

What are your top three achievements in each of the following categories?
- *Career/ professional*
- *Family*
- *Sport / hobbies*
- *Creative*
- *Financial*

*What are your most memorable success **celebrations** so far in life?*

LIFE'S SCORECARD

Life's significant milestones often do not seem like achievements at all, but rather are extraordinary moments in a person's life that we experience in wonder. These might include a first job, a first date, an engagement, a wedding, the birth of a child, or moving to the other side of the world. Some of these moments have an inherent celebration built in (like a wedding), while others might need a moment to pause and consider the meaning of the situation. Often, we do not realise the profound significance until years later when we have experienced the long-term benefit of a meaningful life choice.

Celebrations vary in terms of quality, purpose, or the benefits when considering an achievement versus a life milestone. While there is anxiety inherent in some situations (e.g., proposing to someone), the moment creates a memory for a lifetime that both people can draw on. The wedding ceremony itself is a celebration, most often in the presence of our closest family and friends, and the reception becomes a celebration of a new union and a positive memory for everyone who attends.

It may be helpful to consider the people you have touched and the legacy you have left along the way. Earning a degree may be valuable and set you on a positive career path, but the friendships built along the way are just as meaningful.

My wife often says, "The most important decision you will ever make is choosing the person you will marry [if you choose to marry]!". Falling in love with someone is less of an achievement than a force of nature, but the positive energy and effort that goes into staying married is something to be celebrated. Anniversaries (of your wedding day or the day you met) often act as natural events to reflect on the ups and downs of married life, and to celebrate the joint achievements created on the journey together.

Similarly, children's birthdays may not only be a wonderful celebration of a young person's life, but also may bring back memories of the joy and the stress of the birthing event itself. I witnessed both an emergency and a planned caesarean section during the births of our two boys, and each event brings back specific emotions and memories that capture those moments. The song that was playing during my eldest son's birth still brings a tear to my eye when I hear it on the radio (*If You're Not the One* by Daniel Bedingfield). The whole family often laughs at the memory of this son who, aged five, nearly dropped his grandparents' mobile phone down a drain when he took the call to be told about his baby brother's arrival!

Any birthday can be deemed significant, but there are often coming-of-age milestones that get celebrated more than others. Becoming a teenager or being allowed to drive or to drink legally may lead to extra celebration or significance for everyone witnessing the coming of age. These celebrations often double as important rites of passage, signifying that a child is now an adult, and (usually) wishes to be treated as one. The value of a birthday may lie in reaching a milestone (any milestone), and reflecting on the progress made through life, surrounded and supported by family and loved ones.

These natural family events get celebrated annually, often with the people who attended in the first place, either in person or via warm messages and cards marking the occasion. The moments of celebration foster connection with wider family and friends. Maintaining and strengthening relationships play a significant role in annual celebrations and can be separated from the many commercial messages that become the focus of major holidays. Christmas, Thanksgiving, Easter, birthdays, national holidays (July 1st in Canada and Waitangi Day in New Zealand, for example) give cause to pause and feel grateful for all the people in your life along with the benefits of living in a society to feel proud of, perhaps not all the time, but more often than not. The topic of gratitude will be expanded upon in Chapter 9.

What achievements deserve more recognition or acknowledgement in your life thus far?

MOMENTS OF SUCCESS – WITH AND WITHOUT FULFILMENT, INSPIRATION, AND HAPPINESS

While moments of success can often stand on their own, and be celebrated appropriately, there can be varying degrees of connection to fulfilment, inspiration, and happiness. The FISH experience may influence how or when an achievement may get celebrated, or whether it gets celebrated at all!

Success may arrive accompanied by fulfilment, inspiration, or happiness, but it does not always happen that way. There are countless examples of individuals achieving massive financial success and remaining miserable in their personal life. Or the deep sadness and sometimes despair that comes from losing a loved one, and the guilt associated with the financial freedom created by a life insurance policy. Not every moment of success can be expressed as a positive on all levels.

Success is often richer, or may feel more significant, when fulfilment, inspiration, or happiness co-exist in the build-up to or in the moment of it. Some of my earliest career moments in the pharmaceutical industry felt enormously important (fulfilment) not just to me personally in my career development, but for the health of the nation we were serving at the time. In fact, during the launch of the U.K.'s first over-the-counter emergency contraceptive pill, the significance of the freedom to choose a course of action for women, and the reduction in the number of health professional hurdles to go through, was a powerful moment of change which has since spread globally.

LIFE LED BY SUCCESS

Success and happiness often go hand in hand, but usually only if we pause long enough to feel grateful for the circumstances that led to our achievement. The bliss of winning a sporting event comes from days and months of training invested, with blood, sweat, and tears expended prior to winning a shiny medal. The moment of winning lasts for only seconds, with the event captured on video or in photos to serve as a memory of the hard work it took to get there. Top athletes may struggle to redirect their achievement-focus once they have retired from their sport. Those who are successful usually find a new interest or career to invest in and apply their achievement orientation to that.

Success found in the absence of fulfilment, inspiration, or happiness may feel shallow or even hollow, with little meaning derived from each achievement. For example, winning a silver medal through effort, blood, sweat, and tears at a significant championship may out-shine the triumph of a gold in subsequent years that took significantly less effort or personal investment. However, if you stop to look at an achievement, even one that on the surface might have been a disappointment, you may be able to find nuggets of fulfilment, inspiration, or happiness if you look hard enough. Taking time to reflect on how you have made a difference (fulfilment), how you have done it your own way (inspiration), or the sheer joy you experienced through the accomplishment (happiness) may help bring richness to each experience.

When might you have been caught up in the success hamster wheel, repeating achievement after achievement with no time to reflect on progress?

MOMENT OF COMPLETION VERSUS ENJOYING THE JOURNEY

From my earlier list of categories outlining some of the characteristics of success, it is apparent that success may be enjoyed in a single moment (e.g., winning a sporting event), or by appreciating the journey it took to get there (e.g., the hard work, the training, the strategy, understanding your competition, etc.). Both are rewarding and meaningful, and, in most cases, you can't have one without the other.

In the absence of a *moment of success* (e.g., winning), the journey becomes all the more important to acknowledge and celebrate. In fact, moments of loss may bring deep learning and insight about what not to do in the future, and it would be a mistake to gloss over or forget those experiences.

SUCCESS ACCORDING TO VIDEO GAMES

I am sure that the video game industry is largely built on basic human needs for success, learning, and entertainment. Every game has a learning curve and, with enough practice, mastering a particular game leads to a constant stream of success, either against the game itself (i.e., getting to new levels) or against increasingly challenging opponents (i.e., skill-based matchmaking). Games that lose popularity generally do so as a result of most players reaching a level of mastery that no longer becomes challenging to maintain. This helps explain new game modes and new seasons of popular games such as *Fortnite* and *Fall Guys*. Head-to-head sporting games maintain their popularity due to the thrill of competing against players around the world, and with skill-based matchmaking, always participating in a match that feels both challenging and winnable. Tournaments create the investment of playing to a high standard over a prolonged period, making the reward of becoming champion all the more sweet.

There are interesting generational differences in attitudes to video gaming. Younger generations tend to view it as appropriate entertainment, or even as a new platform for global community. Older generations may view it as a waste of time. Given that gaming and streaming are relatively new industries, it might benefit parents or grandparents to reflect on what pastimes were deemed a "waste of time" by their parents.

Although the video game industry receives much attention for the role it may play in encouraging violence, many games are now being appreciated for the positive impacts they can have. Recent research has begun to focus on how the critical thinking skills learned from playing video games can be translated into real-world skills. A long-term study by Adachi and Willoughby in 2013 found that "The more adolescents that reported playing strategic video games, (e.g., roleplaying games), the more improvements were evident in self-reported problem-solving skills the next year". This in turn led to better school grades.

SUCCESS LINKED TO FI_H

The power and significance of an achievement can be augmented by combining it with fulfilment, inspiration, and happiness. Making a big difference to oneself, to others, or to society more widely (fulfilment) can make an achievement become a legacy.

Doing something unique or new (inspiration) may also create a meaningful achievement, if only by undertaking the accomplishment for the first time or in a new way. A year of marginal improvements or achievements that led to significant life learning remains time well spent, and the investment may pay off sometime in the future. For example, my career hasn't seen an immediate change recently, but I read a lot on topics that have the potential to lift my career in the future if I apply the learnings well.

Experiencing pleasure (happiness) from an achievement often contributes to the joy of success, and when a success becomes too repetitive, the pleasurable feelings may wane. Pursuing a passion or a personal joy is never time wasted; the pleasure from the activity has its own purpose and direction.

Success in the absence of fulfilment, inspiration, and happiness may still create progress, but without any meaning, new experience, or pleasure, that success is less likely to be repeated for sheer lack of motivation and drive to invest in its reoccurrence. This begins to explain the lack of joy or fulfilment people experience when they climb a career ladder or invest in serial entrepreneurship, only to arrive at a point in their life and ask, "Was it all worth it?" or "Where to from here?".

When have you experienced the power of success combined with fulfilment, inspiration, and/or happiness?

When might you have experienced success in the absence of FI_H?

QUICK WINS AND LIFETIME PURSUITS

Time taken to achieve an accomplishment may determine the strength of the feeling of success. The time taken should include all of the preparation and training that went into each success, and the magnitude of change in a person's life that the achievement may create. The list below offers some examples of different scales of accomplishments over time.

Short term:

* Cleaning your house/room and enjoying the result.
* Beating your son at his favourite PlayStation game.
* Walking the dog on a particularly beautiful day.
* Writing a few paragraphs/pages of your book in an afternoon.
* Making that sales call that you have been putting off.
* Completing your monthly invoicing.

Medium term:

* Reviewing your business' strategic plan and acknowledging the progress made in the last 90 days (along with key learnings and insights).
* Painting a room in your house and feeling proud of the change.
* Booking and taking a holiday out of well-earned savings.
* Training intensely for three months in the lead up to a national sporting championship.

Long term:

* Saving a deposit for your first house.
* Earning the next promotion through hard work and dedication to new learning.
* Having the discipline to save for retirement so you can have the funds to make many of your bucket list items come true.

* Building momentum, discipline, and inspiration to write and launch a book.
* Planning and saving for a one-year (or more) gap in your career to do something you really love.

In some cases, achievements are years in the making (e.g., saving for your first home, or building professional reputation and skills toward that next promotion) and no one thing can be pointed at as the reason for the success. Rather, a consistency of investment (saving a little each month or investing in learning and development courses) over time becomes critical to achieving a worthwhile outcome. These longer-term achievements are perhaps more rewarding, as they take a different level of discipline and commitment to bring to fruition. They are also like a muscle, the more you achieve, the more you feel capable of performing in the future.

What are some of your personal and professional short-, medium-, and long-term successes?

What level of focus and talent were required to invest in the longer-term successes?

INSTANT AND DELAYED GRATIFICATION

Coupled with the concept of success invested over time is the dilemma between instant and delayed gratification. It's important to find a balance between investing in celebrations throughout life when they are warranted, and saving or planning for the future in order to achieve things that can only be done over a long period of time. It is not either-or; it's both!

A spontaneous dinner out to celebrate a recent success at work might be appropriate if not for the sunny holiday that you are saving for to experience some well-earned rest and relaxation. Posting record profits in a quarter means very little if some of those funds are not reinvested in the employees through an event or shared profit scheme. Eating cake to celebrate a birthday is fun, but eating cake every day isn't usually in our best interest physically or psychologically.

Studies have shown that children faced with the opportunity to treat themselves immediately to a cookie or wait long enough to receive a second cookie will unearth a success mindset. Those willing to wait were deemed much more likely to be successful in the future, with a built-in discipline towards delayed gratification.

Perhaps hedonism or the pursuit of pleasure is the enemy of building a true legacy which requires an investment over a much longer period of time.

What was the proudest moment of your life so far? What contributed to this moment?

What are you willing to persevere with, learn, study, sacrifice and love in order to accomplish what you truly desire?

> *Success is no accident. It is hard work, perseverance, learning, studying, sacrifice and most of all, love of what you are doing or learning to do. – Pelé*

CHAPTER 7

Defining Wealth

If I were a rich man
Ya ba dibba dibba dibba dibba dibba dibba dum
All day long, I'd biddy biddy bum
If I were a wealthy man.

"If I Were a Rich Man", *Fiddler on the Roof*

ALL THIS TALK about success, achievement and values loses some significance if we don't discuss one of the biggest measures of these three – wealth. Wealth is the outcome of success, having wealth is often ranked as an achievement, and things having value is synonymous with wealth. Yet, what is wealth, really? And how does it fit into our lives?

A DIFFERENCE OF DEFINITIONS

Wealth can be an uncomfortable topic. People want it, but they also don't want to show that they want it. It's not seen as noble to want to be wealthy. This can lead to internal conflict and unnecessary stress. Yet most of this tension comes from a misunderstanding of what wealth is, rather than from the wealth itself.

Wealth – dictionary definitions:

1) An abundance of valuable possessions or money.
    "He used his considerable wealth to bribe officials."
2) Plentiful supply of a particular desirable thing.
    "The tables and maps contain a wealth of information."

Wealth – the *FISH* definition:

1) An abundance of everything you ever wished for.
    "With everything she had in her life, she had wealth beyond measure."

Most people associate wealth with money or financial affluence, but this is a very narrow definition. It omits the possibility of being wealthy in life while lacking in material things, and fails to recognise that many people living "in wealth" are not wealthy at all. This chapter aims to explore the most expansive definition of wealth – receiving an abundance of everything you ever wished for, whatever that might entail. Wealth might also be strongly connected to gratitude or having a deep appreciation for the people and things in your life.

When we consider our wish list of everything we might want, it is easy to dream up material possessions such as cars, houses, money, fancy holidays, etc. It can be more illuminating to build a list of all the non-material things you might want in life, such as friendships, adventure, opportunities to learn, compassion, and – perhaps above all – love.

What is it you truly want out of the remainder of your life? What would you like more of? What would you like less of?

Although creative and financial freedom – the values most easily associated with the common definition of wealth – do feature in my list of values, there are several more essential elements to my life that I rank higher. I would not sacrifice any of these in favour of material wealth. This helps me focus on the people (e.g., family) and things (e.g., health and well-being) that truly matter, with financial wealth being simply a scorecard used to keep track of progress along the way. Similarly, many of my other values that outrank creative and financial freedom are states of being, or behaviours that I intend to follow with or without a lot of material wealth. "Life is fun and easy", "Honour the evolution", and "Live life out loud" can all be experienced with or without lots of money in the bank, and will keep me grounded during periods of feast and famine.

Compare your wish list with your core values from Chapter 3. How well do these align?

_____

_____

_____

How much quality time do you allocate to investing in the core values that are most important to you?

_____

_____

_____

MONEY WON'T BUY YOU HAPPINESS, BUT IT SURE BUYS A LOT OF CHOICES

Several studies worldwide have demonstrated that money, above a certain basic limit, does not buy you happiness. Once we have our core needs met (food, shelter, transportation, entertainment) the incremental gains from having more money seem to pale into insignificance. The very rich are not immune to sadness, depression or discontent, especially if they have not explored their core purpose or key contribution in life. The very rich are often prone to experiencing deficiencies in FISH, which begs the question of the value of a materially abundant life.

The value of a materially abundant life lies in the number of choices one can make in the name of expression, entertainment, or contribution. With low abundance, people often feel trapped and have to expend an enormous amount of energy down one or two paths to create a difference in their lives. With material wealth comes more options, lots of pathways open up, some of which have the potential to make us happy, fulfilled, or both, and if one choice fails to do so, we can re-invest in another one.

My own risk-taking was shaped by the financial security I've felt throughout my life. Moves from Canada to the U.K., and then from the U.K. to New Zealand were preceded by a period of financial and emotional security, making it easy for me to "take a risk". During the move to New Zealand, we were psychologically full of adventure and, in retrospect, had sufficient monetary wealth to bridge the gap that is created when you move to the other side of the world with no employment absolutes planned.

The risk paid off, with us both securing new jobs, Fiona as a family lawyer having requalified into New Zealand law, and I had the courage to re-invent myself out of the pharmaceutical industry and into a role as a business development coach in Wellington. We have never looked back.

Nearly every big decision we've made has involved a six-month savings safety net that has given us breathing space to make mistakes and change course if we needed to. Starting my own business following 22 years of employment was another example of this. Fiona and I consciously saved about six months' salary to assist us in the event that my business was not able to support our outgoings adequately. Mentally, the freedom this created for me was strong enough to take calculated risks and push myself into the marketplace as a business coach and mentor in ways I perhaps would not have done if fear had been the back-drop to my decisions.

When have you benefited from the freedom to take risks, perhaps due to a financial safety net?

When has material wealth allowed you to pursue options you might not have taken otherwise?

NIGEL LATTA'S FINANCIAL MODEL

Nigel Latta's *Money Personality* model is one of the most useful models I have come across regarding financial risk-taking. This model breaks people down into four distinct personalities, each with strengths and weaknesses:

Freedom seekers
These people value experiences, living in the moment, and using their money for things that they are passionate about. The

strength of this personality is the ability to find great happiness. They risk not putting aside resources for their own futures.

Security savers

People with this money personality value finances as a way to be safe and in control. They are often focused more on the home than on the outside world. Strengths of this type are great preparedness for the future, while a weakness is missing out on experiences in the present.

Sociable sharers

If you're in this category, you demonstrate love for others through the way you spend money. You may be stingy about spending on yourself, but utterly generous when it comes to looking after friends. Strengths of the sociable sharer are using money as an active part of relationship building and mainte-nance. A weakness may be spending too much on others and not leaving enough for your own future.

Power spenders

Those who find themselves with a power spender mentality tend to use money to make an impression, demonstrate status, or create a feeling for themselves. Strengths of the power spender are fearlessness about risk-taking and investments. A weakness is a tendency towards buying for the sake of buying, without genuine appreciation of the purchases.

Which money personality feels like a "best fit" for you?

What are the benefits and risks attached to this personality type?

MORE TO LIFE THAN MONEY

Having an abundance of material things may bring a certain sense of security, privilege, and opportunity to your life, but I would wager most of us would trade it all in for more of the intangibles. Relationships in particular provide us with friendship, support, encouragement, and love.

It is remarkable how often people get stuck in the pursuit of more possessions (versus more experiences or more relationships). How often do we measure our success by our annual salary increase or promotion, rather than the number of lives we've touched? We forget that relationship emotions are always reciprocal – the energy I put into supporting others is most often reflected in the support I receive in return. The friendship and encouragement I invest in is returned by those I am connected to and place value in. The love I bring to my most important relationships is reflected back at me, often augmented in ways I can only dream of and feel grateful for. Seemingly, the more I give, the more I get back in return.

Non-relational values can also be a source of abundance, such as freedom to choose, experiencing adventure, and opportunities to learn. The emotions associated with these can exist regardless of the scale of material wealth you might be experiencing, as most are dictated by mindset first and foremost. In fact, many of these states of mind are sources of your ability to generate material wealth. For example, a growth or learning mindset will tackle new challenges and add new value to the world around you, resulting in a greater return on investment. Or a sense of adventure and risk-taking may result in taking a leap of faith when it is most needed, leading to the next big opportunity of your career.

Which non-relational values are you prioritising in your life right now?

_____

_____

_____

How are they poised to help you succeed in the future?

_____

_____

RESOURCES VERSUS RESOURCEFULNESS

In terms of wealth and abundance, the contributors to our success may stem from resources (external) or resourcefulness (internal). Many employee engagement tools often get hung up on the resources needed to do the job, but fail to acknowledge or support the resourcefulness required to excel in a given role.

Resources might include a laptop to work on, the budget available, or even colleagues on hand to support the project.

Resourcefulness might include resilience on any given day, the strength of internal and external relationships, or powers of persuasion in lobbying for more resources to get the job done. Very few "employee engagement" tools focus enough on the resourcefulness of their employees to make a meaningful difference to their lives and their ability to thrive on the job.

How would you rate your level of resources and resourcefulness in comparison to what you need to get your most important projects done (personal or professional)?

When has your resourcefulness been strong enough to overcome or compensate for a lack of resources?

INFINITE ABUNDANCE

There is a big difference in mindsets between believing you have everything you need to succeed, and focusing on what you lack (or on what is preventing you from succeeding). Further to the last section on resourcefulness, believing that anything is possible and that there is always a way forward will drive an individual to solve nearly any problem and achieve their objective. If we contrast that language with "I never have enough", or "If only I had…", it becomes obvious why some people achieve outcomes that others cannot.

We all have the same number of hours in the day, and yet, some people seem to be inherently more productive or impactful in the world. Perhaps it is because of the opportunity they see, and the belief that it is up to them to unlock that opportunity.

In the realm of infinite abundance, a guiding philosophy is the principle that we will always have everything we need to accomplish a goal or objective, even if the source of the resources/ resourcefulness may be hidden or delayed. Key questions that come from an abundant mindset include, "What do I need more of to accomplish my objective? Who can help? Why is this barrier meant to be overcome, and how will I overcome it?".

Imagine that you had everything you needed to succeed at whatever you wished to accomplish. How would that level of abundance feel?

How certain would you be of your success? Specifically, what will you do differently to move one step closer to your objective? If you are meant to be successful, who and what do you need in your life to make that success a reality?

DREAMING OF FUTURE PROSPERITY VERSUS APPRECIATING EVERYTHING YOU HAVE TODAY

We face a balancing act: wishing for more in life in the future while simultaneously loving and appreciating everything we have right now. Our hopes and dreams are built on wishing for more or different than what we have today. Those feelings are essential for making progress and we would not continuously improve our lives were it not for hopes and dreams.

Translating hopes and dreams into reality requires more concrete goals and intentions. We need to take action towards the future state we are dreaming of. Rhonda Byrne's bestselling book, *The Secret,* suggests using "Ask, believe, receive" as a formula for getting what you wish for. I've used her formula as a base for what I'd recommend:

* Ask for what you wish for and deeply visualise it.
* Believe that you have already received it.
* **Act fiercely in pursuit of your wish and employ every strategy you can imagine to achieve it.**
* Receive what you have wished for.

Step three is often missed out of law of attraction literature, and I have often wondered, "How does the Universe know what to deliver if you don't give it a clue along the way? Why should the Universe deliver if we won't demonstrate commitment to the process?".

The balancing act is to have these aspirations AND be secure and happy with everything you have in the present. Our gratitude for what we have will give us confidence that we can seek and secure new things in the future, be they material, relational, or experiential. The foundation for actualising a future dream is to understand and believe that the dream we are currently living was crafted some time ago, and that all our dreams are currently coming true as we designed years ago. The future consequence of our current dream will be revealed in due course.

What are your hopes, dreams, goals, and intentions?
Which dream would you prioritise actualising in the next
12 months?

> *Plant seeds of happiness, hope, success, and love; it*
> *will all come back to you in abundance.*
>
> — Steve Maraboli

CHAPTER 8

Pursuing a Greatest Imaginable Challenge

There's always gonna be another mountain,
I'm always gonna wanna make it move,
Always gonna be an uphill battle
Sometimes I'm gonna have to lose.
Ain't about how fast I get there,
Ain't about what's waiting on the other side,
It's the climb.

"The Climb" – Jessi Alexander and Jon Mabe

A T THE JUNCTION of our passions, what we do best and where we add the most value to ourselves and others, lies our Greatest Imaginable Challenge (GIC). In Jim Collins' exceptional book *Good to Great*, he discusses "Big Hairy Audacious Goals" (BHAG's) for organisations; the Greatest Imaginable Challenge is a personal and individual pursuit along the same lines.

Think of a Greatest Imaginable Challenge as a goal or intention to be experienced over a long period of time, perhaps a lifetime. Consider the pursuit of it as the goal itself. It represents your personal Mount Everest, to be climbed from base camp to summit, and perhaps beyond, experiencing and relishing every milestone along the way. This, really, is what we are on earth to do. To think up audacious, awe-inspiring challenges, and to go out and meet them head on. Some will be highly visible; others will be subtle, slow-growth movements. We all have the seeds of a GIC (or two!) inside us.

DISCOVERING YOUR OWN GREATEST IMAGINABLE CHALLENGE

To begin discovering what your Greatest Imaginable Challenge(s) might be, ask yourself the following questions and document your answers in a journal or notepad.

What are you most passionate about in work and life?

When have you been at your very best? What were you doing?

Where have you added the most value to yourself or others?

Expanding on these initial questions, consider the following:

What do you love doing most?

_____

_____

_____

What aspirations have you had for your life, in the past and the present?

_____

_____

_____

What exceptional talents do you have that propel you to success?

_____

_____

_____

How do you typically measure the value you deliver to yourself or bring to others?

_____

_____

_____

Your level of ambition may influence the scale of the challenge you choose to pursue, but it will nearly always be entirely personal to you, and your motivation to complete the challenge largely comes from within.

FIONA'S GREATEST IMAGINABLE CHALLENGES

My role model for the achievement of Greatest Imaginable Challenges is my wife, Fiona. While I have spent a lifetime investing in goal-setting and achieving processes, my wife seems to glide with ease from one major achievement to another, smiling and laughing every step of the way. Fiona made me realise the difference between a goal and an intention. While a goal is a hope with a deadline in the future, for Fiona her intentions have already occurred when she envisions them. There is no possibility of failure, because deep down she has already committed herself to the journey of achieving each intention.

The very first example of this occurred when my wife woke up one morning in Edinburgh and, over breakfast, proceeded to announce the fact that she intended to cycle from Land's End to John O'Groats, the length of the United Kingdom from south to north. At the time, she had a love of cycling (one of her passions), however, she in no way was cycling distances that might justify her commitment to cycle the length of Britain. Very calmly and in a focused way, Fiona set aside time each day to plan her training, her route up the country, accommodation for us as a family as we traversed the nation, and even her daily diet to get her to the end.

At the heart of this Greatest Imaginable Challenge lay the following key elements:

* Passion – Fiona loved cycling solo; no need for a peloton, just her and her bike.

* Do best – Fiona finishes everything she starts; once she

put her mind to this ride, very little was going to get in her way.

❧ Add value – Fiona's self-assurance is enhanced each time she accomplishes a new challenge. She also loves the process of getting fitter through disciplined exercise (this was no charity cycle; it was done for pure self-improvement and the experience).

Weeks of training and planning led to a start-gun in Land's End, Cornwall on the 23rd of July, 2007. Every day, three-year-old Cameron and I dropped Fiona off for her day of cycling, and every evening we would pick her up to take her to our pre-arranged hostel or bed and breakfast, only to return her the very next morning. Through scorching sun and torrential rain, Fiona made her way up the country one day at a time. We celebrated on the 2nd of August when she crossed the border into Scotland, and celebrated again on the 8th when she and a friend rode into John O'Groats in the northeast corner of Scotland. What did she get out of it? Seventeen days of cycling, one day of rest, the Scottish leg accompanied by a friend, with the rest done entirely solo, for the sheer bliss of it, and to be able to say she had done it.

Not content with one GIC that year, Fiona embarked on two more:

* Emigrating from Scotland to New Zealand.
  * Passion: experiencing new places.
  * Do best: follow through on a sense of adventure.
  * Add value: promise of an exceptional place to bring up a family.

* Requalifying into New Zealand law (six exams, all administered remotely).
  * Passion: love of learning.
  * Do best: always finishes what she starts.
  * Add value: capacity to earn as a fully qualified family lawyer in New Zealand.

The most important philosophy that Fiona has adopted through all of her Greatest Imaginable Challenges, one that will benefit anyone setting out on their own GIC, is to choose an objective, activity, or experience that you will enjoy for every single moment, even under the most difficult circumstances.

FUTURE-FOCUSED GREATEST IMAGINABLE CHALLENGES

My own Greatest Imaginable Challenges are strongly future-focused, and informed by my personal working, sporting, and health histories.

Towards the end of a twelve-year sales and marketing career

in pharmaceutical and biotech management, I had the opportunity to enhance my management skills by attending a course that introduced me to the art and science of coaching. I immediately fell in love with the spirit of coaching and, following that employer-sponsored course, pursued a Personal Performance Coaching Certificate and Diploma in Corporate and Executive Coaching with The Coaching Academy in the United Kingdom. The timing of these courses coincided with our family's decision to emigrate to New Zealand, and the opportunity arose to redefine my career entirely.

Upon our arrival in Wellington, I joined a small-business coaching firm (Results.com) and developed a passion for helping small-business owners create businesses to be proud of. Many of the fundamentals from my time at Results are reflected in this book.

Following three years at Results, I had the opportunity to join an international management consulting firm (Gallup), where I led many projects to lift employee engagement and build a strengths-based culture, mostly in very large firms across New Zealand and Australia.

My love of small business never left me, and after a seven-year experience at Gallup, I had the courage to set up my own strengths-based coaching and mentoring practice (originally ChrisMillerCoaching, now ChristopherMiller.co.nz). As I set up my practice, I was inspired to create my own Greatest Imaginable Challenge, which can be summarised as follows:

* Passion: helping New Zealand business owners develop lives and businesses to be proud of.

* Do best: integrated personal, business, and strengths-based coaching.
* Add value: create strategies for defining and lifting fulfilment, inspiration, success, and happiness.

The integration of these three elements led me to the following GIC: "By 2030, significantly influence the success of the New Zealand SME sector and emulate Edwards Deming's impact on Japan after the second world war".

Edwards Deming is the father of Total Quality Management/ Continuous Quality Improvement. He had a profound effect on the manufacturing quality and success of Japanese business over the course of several decades. I love inspiring role models, and would be proud to create an impact as significant as that of Edwards Deming if I can. This GIC may sound overly grand, but just in the act of striving for it, I am certain I will make a difference to those I have the privilege to serve along the way.

SPRINGBOARD SUCCESS

The second of my current Greatest Imaginable Challenges is derived from my love of platform and springboard diving. As a young teenager, I had the opportunity to compete as a springboard diver at the Canada Games. Though I was never exceptional at the sport, I enjoyed the camaraderie and the uniqueness of diving. Every diver knows the fear of learning a new dive, and the pain when the dive goes wrong.

I was proud to dive through to early university, and I competed on the Ontario/Quebec circuit in 1993 and '94. Without any significant competitive aspirations, my diving career went on hold for about 25 years!

Born to a trampolining mother and a diving father, Cameron and Ross had little chance of avoiding a tumbling sport, and after short forays into gymnastics, both have embraced the sport of diving through the fantastic culture of Wellington Diving Club (WDC). Competitive events are a family affair, with both boys competing and me and Fiona judging when we can. Cameron is also an active coach of junior divers in the club. Furthermore, I have contributed to the WDC's committee at various times and love the depth of community support that the club's families offer.

My current GIC for diving feels hugely aspirational. It is influenced by a wide number of people in various leadership roles for the sport.

- Passion: love the art of falling with style.
- Do best: performance coaching and inspiring a common goal.
- Add value: offer my time and expertise, especially to the business of sporting excellence.

My GIC for diving can be summarised as: "To help and support the New Zealand diving community to create at least three World or Olympic medallists by 2030, and sustain this level of achievement for a decade".

MENTAL HEALTH PARADIGM

Sometimes, a Greatest Imaginable Challenge can be very personal *and* have a wider impact on society. I have always felt that my mental health diagnosis and the way I cope with my bipolar condition could serve as a positive role model for others. This led to the following GIC: "Be the catalyst for a paradigm shift in the New Zealand mental health community and society to unlock the vast potential from those who experience, manage and are recovering from mental health conditions".

* Passion: to discover high performance in a life well lived, no matter the conditions or circumstance.
* Do best: "Live life out loud" and be an example where I can.
* Add value: role model life as a high performing bipolar individual, with the courage to do so publicly.

I find this one the most difficult to write and commit to, as it requires a level of vulnerability deeper than I may be capable of.

April 2009 changed my life, and the lives of my family members completely. Accepting a bipolar diagnosis, especially considering the stigma both in wider society and among friends and family, means that this is a condition re-lived over and over again. People's lack of understanding, or their assumption about what you are capable or incapable of achieving creates a hidden barrier that goes beyond the biology of your condition.

I have also found it fascinating to read about the extraordinary links between mental health conditions and excellence in various domains. From business (Ted Turner), to art (van Gogh), to music (Demi Lovato, Mariah Carey) to literature (Ernest Hemingway), to entertainment (Stephen Fry, Carrie Fisher) – the list of culturally significant personalities who have lived with bipolar disorder and thrived is longer than you might imagine.

Much has been written on the links between creativity and depression and/or bipolar. I believe this represents a hidden potential in society for extraordinary contributions to the way we live. My own imagination and creativity go through peaks and trough depending on my medication among other coping mechanisms. Often, my thoughts are characterised by deep insights, either about my own life or about the progress of humanity in some way. Given my brief "God-consciousness" experience at that Tony Robbins event back in April 2009, I am now of the belief that those with mental health conditions have the potential to tap into a level of greater wisdom and connectedness when lucid, that the rest of society struggles to see or experience.

TIME TO SET FORTH ON YOUR OWN!

The spirit of a Greatest Imaginable Challenge can be as big or small as you need it to be. It is meant to be a source of inspiration, usually for you personally or those in your trusted inner circle. Coupled with your sense of purpose, it can act as a guiding light to direct your energy and your talents toward an objective that you deem deeply worthwhile. Try not to judge yourself for what your ambition encourages you to accomplish, or limit your potential in any way.

What is one Greatest Imaginable Challenge that is hiding at the back of your mind?

What would happen if you gave yourself permission to pursue it?

As you will have seen, particularly from the examples provided through Fiona's stories, you are not restricted to having only one Greatest Imaginable Challenge. If this were the case, my goodness, you'd never get started for fearing of using it up! Throw those fears away. Both Fiona and I have had a great variety of GICs, each relevant to our life stages and desires. Your own GICs may be academic, creative, sporting, intellectual, social, or community-based. You may have three in the same category, building off each other. You may have five in five different life areas! There are no limits. Dream big, and then live your dreams.

What are three more Greatest Imaginable Challenges that you could see yourself doing in the future?

INTERMISSION

My wife, Fiona Lindsey Miller, sadly passed away in July 2021. The preceding eight chapters were written while she was still alive, and benefited from her valuable insight and wisdom. The following five chapters were written after she passed, and the subject matter and writing is both raw and filled with emotion as a result of substantial grief.

Initially, I planned to go back and rewrite the first eight chapters to correct the tense, communicating to readers that my wife was no longer alive. But I realised that the best demonstration of the value of FISH would involve showing what it is like to apply these lessons not only in the best of times, but also in the worst. These were the words, thoughts, and feelings that I had as I wrote the first eight chapters, and I did not want to hide them from the world. I hope that the truth of this can be a beacon for others in their times of need.

Through this astoundingly difficult time, my measures of fulfilment, inspiration, success and happiness served as a compass for me more than ever. FISH doesn't rely on everything working out the way you wanted it to – not at all. FISH is about living a meaningful and wonderful life, no matter what challenges you pass through.

CHAPTER 9

Navigating Resilience

What doesn't kill you makes you stronger
Stand a little taller
Doesn't mean I'm lonely when I'm alone.

Stronger – Kelly Clarkson

THE JOY OF finding FISH is not merely about finding and labelling the good things in the good moments of life. It is about understanding the beauty and growth that can be found in all moments of life. It is about using FISH to come out stronger from hard times, to build your character over time and through challenges. Not only is FISH something to find joy in, it is also a powerful tool for resilience.

FROM VULNERABILITY TO RESILIENCE

Resilience is the ability to survive, thrive or maintain a high level of performance in the face of substantial obstacles, stress, or personal tragedy.

It is rather ironic that to build resilience, we must also experience our most vulnerable selves. We create a more resilient self when we come out the other side of a challenge or crisis. When we are *in* the crisis, we are usually unaware that resilience is being built or strengthened, we are simply focused on survival or coping the best we can with the resources and resourcefulness we have.

Our level of resilience for meeting the next challenge in our life is built upon our cumulative previous experiences, especially the crises or tragedies that we have survived and, in some cases, thrived through. Subconsciously, we seem to be able to remember that if we survived the previous situation, then we can find the energy to cope with the one in front of us. The dilemma is, each situation is new and brings its own challenges, but our coping mechanisms largely remain the same. Sometimes, a crisis arises that is so completely foreign or shocking that you are forced to learn new strategies to survive.

FINDING RESILIENCE IN MYSELF

In the aftermath of losing my wife and life partner, Fiona, to cancer, I have never felt so fragile or devastated. I had few reference points to cope with such an enormous loss, with most family members previously living long and fruitful lives before passing away. The first three months especially were incredibly lonely and sorrowful, with many friends reluctant or unsure of how to support me. Coping involved doing the basics day in and day out – get up, shower, breakfast, walk the dog, take the boys to school, laundry, vacuum, take the boys to diving, cook dinner. Just being required to do these things meant I had to engage in life, though productivity otherwise was very low.

As the months passed, somehow, I created more capacity for creativity and commitment to my family and clients. I began engaging with the people I trusted most, who had sympathy or especially empathy for my situation. A very small number of them were willing to take a risk on my coaching and mentoring skills despite my grief, or perhaps because of my grief, and I will always be grateful to them. Family also rallied round to support me when I needed it most, and though they sometimes struggled to understand what I was going through, they were always there for me unconditionally.

My resilience came in the form of being able to do normal things and let grief sit beside me through the process. Fiona's absence is palpable, and at times the grief and pain are physical, usually in my gut and my heart. Concentrating on taking big, deep breaths will often reduce the intensity of the pain, but there are days when I have cried so hard and so much that I stopped breathing from the sheer weight of my grief.

Each new day and week following Fiona's passing brought new strength. My first meeting with my business manager, my first face-to-face with a friend, watching my first basketball game with the boys, my first client session, my first new client who had no context about my recent loss, editing my first blog, writing my first new chapter. Each new experience was a milestone to be built on with new realisation about what I was capable of. Even now, I am laying the groundwork for a much more resilient future that has not yet come to pass. I am also sure that I will experience a crisis in the future, for which losing Fiona has prepared me to cope with.

In my most desperate moments – both during this crisis and in the past – I have asked, "Why me?", and the only answer that keeps coming back is "Because I can." I can survive this. I can cope with this. I can find a way forward, no matter how hard life gets. I do not know what the future will hold, but I know that my past and my present have prepared me as best they can for what I have yet to face.

ASSESSING YOUR OWN RESILIENCE-BUILDING MOMENTS

Throughout our lives, each of us will face challenges and incur traumas, both big and small. Being brave enough to face these moments and to look back on them will likely unearth pivotal experiences that are worth drawing learnings from. We all tend to repeat the same behaviours in challenging situations until we are mature and aware enough to learn and change. Making this an active process is worthwhile.

Challenges and traumas always bring with them deep accompanying feelings. There may be anger or sadness in your past. There may be shame in actions you took or the way you responded to something. There may be disappointment or missed opportunities. There may be relationships that broke down, or people who hurt you. Being able to look *at* these feelings – as opposed to feeling them directly – is one step in the process of understanding and growing.

What are the top three challenging moments of your life so far?

_____

_____

_____

How have they prepared you for the future?

_____

_____

_____

What did you learn about yourself that you didn't know before?

_____

_____

_____

You'll likely find some internal resistance to the idea of viewing challenging moments as positives, especially if you are currently in the middle of one. This is normal and understandable. You may still find something useful comes out of working through these questions. Equally, you may want to think back to a less recent or less painful challenging moment to get started. Either way, the fact that there is resistance says only that you are still growing from this experience; allow and accept this. You don't have to bounce back from something immediately. You don't have to have already built resilience. This is a slow and hard process, one that will continue throughout your life.

What thoughts or issues come to mind when you consider resilience in your own life? How easy is it for you to access and remember previous traumatic or challenging events in your life and consider how these have shaped you as a person?

SEEKING PLEASURE

A great coach once told me that humans have been built to do two things – seek pleasure and avoid pain, and that most human behaviour can be explained by one or the other. Perhaps resilience can also be seen through this lens. In the act of avoiding or confronting pain, or building our emotional muscle in the pursuit of pleasure, we will unknowingly increase our resilience, and be more prepared for future obstacles or opportunities. The energy we spend in avoiding or navigating our way out of pain creates new coping mechanisms and a level of resourcefulness that we didn't know we had. Once pain has been navigated, our pursuit of pleasure inspires us to make constant and never-ending changes, seeking our next best moment in life.

Seeking pleasure can be a strong motivator for making life better day to day and week to week. Finding new ways to make life fun and easy can be a game worth playing, and one that can be shared with others by helping them find pleasure in life. The danger comes when your pleasure is at the expense of other people's pain or hardship, or the scale of your pleasure becomes foreign to most other people on the planet (think *The Wolf of Wall Street*). Seek pleasure until hedonism kicks in.

One way to remain focused on your future pleasures is to keep an up-to-date bucket list of your hopes and dreams. This can be divided into the following sections (inspired by Louise Hay):

* What would I like to have in the future?
* What would I like to be in the future?
* What would I like to do in the future?
* What would I like to give back in the future?

Have may represent material things you would like to acquire, or emotions you would like to experience along the way. *Be* can mean anything you'd like to become, which may entail a new career, new knowledge, a new volunteer role, new training, etc. *Do* involves the experiences you would like to have – travel, learn a new sport, or spend time in nature, for example. And *give back* is your contribution to others by sharing your time, talents, or treasures.

Do you find it easy to seek pleasure? What are some of your hopes and dreams?

AVOIDING PAIN

In principle, avoiding pain is a useful strategy, until we need a new challenge in life. Many people make what seem to be crazy career decisions, such as changing industries or careers, or starting their own business, all in the hopes of a better future (pleasure), but also in the avoidance of a current career situation that they have already mastered, or become dissatisfied with. Equally, many people become stuck in a job that they dislike, because they fear the pain of leaving and starting anew. Boredom especially can inspire a change when an individual feels a risk is worth taking, even if there might be some pain involved, like retraining or learning a new industry.

Life has a funny way of delivering new pain when we get too comfortable. Just when we think everything is going smoothly, a challenge will come out of nowhere and blindside us. It might be life's way of saying, "You're getting complacent, here's an extra hurdle to overcome".

What lengths do you go to in avoiding pain? In what area of your life could you embrace pain better?

TAKING CALCULATED RISKS

When considering a major life changing decision (such as changing careers, moving countries, choosing a life partner, etc.) it might be worth taking a calculated risk. This useful concept is about weighing the risks and benefits of both following through with the decision and/or maintaining the status quo (an equally valid decision). It's about taking a risk after you've calculated what might come from it. Questions to consider include:

* What are the potential consequences of this decision?
* What could be the upsides of making a change?
* What are the benefits of remaining where I am (no decision)?
* What are the downsides of remaining where I am?
* Why am I ready to make this decision now?
* Why is now not the right time to decide? What additional information do I need?

In the end, if the perceived benefits outweigh the potential downsides, a decision is worth taking. It's also worth noting that a change of circumstance usually leads to unforeseen upsides too.

Where necessary, it might be worth finding ways to mitigate

risk to commit to the decision. For example, before leaving 22 years of employment to set up my own business, we consciously saved more than six months' salary to create a cushion in case my coaching/mentoring practice did not thrive as quickly as expected. About half of that cushion was needed to maintain our financial stability while I became established. Other examples of mitigating risk might include identifying multiple options or backup plans in case your first choice goes wrong for any reason. Investing time in preparation (e.g., for a public speech or training for a sporting final) is generally worthwhile and will build skill and confidence which can come to the fore during the event itself. Tough decisions can be made easier when we take the time to set ourselves up for success.

INSTANT VERSUS DELAYED GRATIFICATION – NO PAIN NO GAIN

There is an argument for investing in pain for the sake of longer-term gain. Delayed gratification usually results in more significant or more satisfying pleasure down the road. There may also be an argument for *acceptable pain* which creates a beneficial outcome in the future. For example, being frugal with money and experiencing austere holidays with the purpose of saving a deposit on a house results in the longer-term outcome of getting on the property ladder and having your own bricks and mortar to improve. Short-term pain for long-term gain.

Resilience may also be viewed through the lens of delayed gratification. Intense training or preparation for a future event involves the intentional building of skill and stamina, leading to an exceptional outcome that may seem easy in comparison to the training that was invested.

INSIGHT AND LEARNING FROM PAIN

In the end, pain serves an important purpose: it can be a powerful motivator for change. Until recently, I hadn't realised the value of sitting with pain, understanding it, welcoming it in, and processing it. It is highly uncomfortable. While we are often taught to avoid or minimise pain through life, sometimes deep pain cannot be avoided, it simply has to be experienced in order to come through the other side.

While pain is not the only way we learn, it might be one of the most powerful ways. Taking an emotional hit, in whatever form, leads to insight, new strength, and a capacity for the future that is difficult to articulate when you are going through a particularly painful event. Perhaps we are the sum of our life's achievements and defeats.

When have you experienced the greatest pain in your life?

What did you learn from the experience?

How have you grown or coped with challenging experiences since?

RESILIENCE ROLE MODELS

I am fortunate enough to have lived with two extraordinary resilience role models – my wife Fiona and my eldest son Cameron. These two individuals have navigated life with an admirable ease. Their approaches to life led me to adopt the core value of "Life is fun and easy", which feels more aspirational at times given the intensity with which I live my life.

Fiona's sense of adventure and fun led her to many of the decisions in her life, including switching degrees in favour of law early in her academic career, driving our immigration to New Zealand from Scotland, and embarking on the adventure of a lifetime in the form of her PhD in law. Her achievements are remarkable in themselves, but even more so given her light-heartedness and the joy she experienced with every decision she made. There were never any regrets.

Fiona's resilience was sorely tested when a client she represented in Wellington was granted a protection order from her husband, which horrifically did not prevent that client from being killed under terrible circumstances. Fiona's recovery from that situation was remarkable, given the relative absence of any professional support, and she went on to record a video of her professional experience in the hopes of helping other lawyers in the future.

Fiona's journey with cancer was also extraordinary. Four days after receiving the diagnosis of her first brain tumour, Fiona underwent brain surgery, and within the following three days was at home recovering. While she received her radiotherapy treatment, she committed herself to swimming the length of New Zealand in our local pools. Within a month of completing radiotherapy, she'd completed 150 lengths in one session and loved every minute. Before she passed away, Fiona completed 65km of swimming on her 1402km quest. Family and friends are intent on completing the swim on her behalf, and in sponsorship of The Neurological Foundation of New Zealand.

Cameron, our eldest son, takes after his mother when it comes to resilience; he has a matter-of-fact way of navigating life that is simultaneously incredibly responsible and low stress. The day Fiona came home from the hospital after her first brain surgery, Cameron committed himself to two hours of chemistry studying in order to feel fully prepared for an exam he had the following week. This came about with no pressure from us, this was entirely his decision and his own self-motivation and desire to meet his own expectations.

Similarly, Cameron came home one day from a three-day high school camp, quickly took a bath, got some food into him and, at 5pm on a Friday, logged on to a university math tutorial for the beginning of his university math curriculum.

Our search for "normal" began quite quickly following Fiona's death and a proud resilient moment occurred five days after her passing. Cameron is the coach of my younger son Ross's basketball team. Both were at their very best that night and Ross earned player of the game. It felt surreal for me to be experiencing normal life, and to have Fiona's presence beside me cheering the boys on.

Who are your resilience role models? Without idolising them, what have you most respected about the way they've dealt with challenges in their lives?

A diamond is just a chunk of coal that did well under pressure. — Henry Kissinger

CHAPTER 10

Gratitude

While it may be easy to feel grateful for the positive things in your life, or when life is running smoothly, could you find gratitude in the midst of a personal crisis or trauma?

Christopher Miller

In this moment, what are you most thankful for? What were you most thankful for when you woke up this morning? What are you most thankful for this year?

T AKING TIME TO reflect on what you are grateful for is becoming more and more common, as people realise the benefit of feeling happy and at peace with the things that add the most value to their lives. Gratitude journals, saying thanks for something or someone, saying grace before a meal, or simply reflecting on the highlights of the day are all becoming more common practice and advocated in wisdom literature, especially in more recent times.

BENEFITS OF GRATITUDE

Once we start experiencing gratitude, the benefits of establishing such a practice become evident. Repetition, or creating a habit, builds gratitude like a muscle and enables the individual to experience moments of peace and happiness that they might not otherwise experience. Positive feelings directed at another person, thing, or situation will often be reflected back to the originator, either in the moment of reflection or at some point in the future.

Feeling grateful during a positive moment is often easy and effortless – we simply appreciate the circumstances we find ourselves in and the serendipity that led to that moment. Yet even this seems to be easier to say than to put into practice. Often, people's lives move fast, and they forget or simply omit the act of stopping to reflect on their moments of gratitude. This omission can lead to a feeling of entitlement, or not appreciating the people and circumstances that contributed positively to your current life. If you feel like you are owed what you receive, you will often neglect all the amazing people and forces that contributed to your positive moment.

Creating a habit of gratitude that is consistent no matter what's going on in our lives can be more challenging, especially when faced with feeling grateful for the mundane or the tragic moments in our lives. It is easy to forget, ignore, or push away thoughts of gratitude. The principles of FISH lend themselves to a habit of gratitude. The positive emotions created by fulfilment, inspiration, success, and happiness can all be augmented by feeling grateful for what led to FISH in the first place.

What was the most memorable positive experience in your life so far?

What do you imagine being most grateful for in ten years' time?

GRATITUDE IN A CRISIS

With the loss of my wife to brain cancer, 2021 quickly became the worst year of my life. However, I was surprised by the clarity that surrounded everything I felt grateful for during this period in my life. There is no way I will ever come to feel remotely grateful for my wife's passing, I am too angry and sad for that to be the case. However, there are many circumstances surrounding her passing that I am unbelievably grateful for.

I will be forever grateful to the team at Mary Potter Hospice for the care, compassion, and dignity with which they treated my wife in her final months of life. That care and compassion extended to us as a family. Without fail, the staff at the hospice treated us all with respect and kindness every single day. I am also grateful that my wife timed her passing to ensure that the boys and I were present during her final hours. I'm deeply thankful that I was holding her hand when she took her final breath.

Since her passing, I have been amazed and grateful for the resilience of Cameron and Ross, and the ease with which they have adapted to normal life without their mother to guide their path. This has included watching them finish high school and intermediate school with great academic and extracurricular success, and witnessing Cameron take control of his future at university, navigating enrolment, scholarship, and residence with ease.

Throughout 2021, I have also been grateful for friends and family, who have rallied around offering support, or sometimes just a listening ear when I needed it most. The loss of a life partner is a foreign and emotional event, for the immediate family as well as the extended circle of friends. Not everyone has behaved as expected, but I am sincerely grateful to those who found a way to try to understand my grief and console it when possible. During my grieving process, I have pulled together a book of memories for Fiona which uniquely summarises the many ways people loved her. Their memories are expressions of gratitude for having known Fiona and been touched by her energy and extraordinary character.

More than anything, losing someone you love makes you deeply grateful for the life you got to share together. I spent just over 24 years with an amazing woman who loved me for who I am every single day. I am grateful for the life we built together, and especially for the two amazing sons we brought into this world.

DEFINING THE WHY OF GRATITUDE

Often, we feel grateful "just because", but it can be powerful to identify the "why" behind the gratitude. Why am I grateful? What purpose does this feeling of gratitude serve? A moment of gratitude goes that little bit deeper when you can identify the reason behind the feeling. Sometimes, appreciating a sunset reminds you of a great day you have had, or valuing the feeling of peace and connection to nature in the moment of the sunset. Perhaps the sunset reminds you of many specific days which ended in a similar way and were worth appreciating.

Feeling grateful for the people around you can also benefit from a deeper explanation. Acknowledging a kindness from someone will often make you realise that they are nearly always kind in some way, or that their kindness reminds you to be kind to others (and to yourself) when the opportunity arises.

While there doesn't have to be a sense of purpose behind a moment of gratitude, sometimes the significance of the moment is powerful and overwhelming. There can be strong emotions when you feel deeply connected to the person or situation that you feel thankful for. Even in the moment of gratitude, you may not be able to explain the magnitude of the significance, but just acknowledge that the moment is meaningful and record it in some way in order to refer back to it in the future.

Who are you particularly grateful for right now? Why are you thankful that they are in your life?

Whose love and support do you value more than any other?

EVIDENCE AND STRENGTHS-BASED COMPLIMENTS

Society often shies away from public displays of appreciation for others. In many cases, a simple thank-you is offered for a helping hand, but the true feeling of thanks is rarely expressed. Wouldn't it be amazing if after every "thank you" came a sincere compliment directed at the person to whom we were thankful? Think of it as "Thank you because…" or "I appreciate you because…".

The key to this working is the authenticity of the compliment; it should be true and natural to that person in that moment, and reflect the very best version of them. Here are a few examples:

"Cameron, thanks for being so proactive around the house and in making big decisions about your future. My own personal stress is much lower as a result, and I am grateful for your independence and maturity."

"Ross, thanks for being so upbeat and positive! Your energy and enthusiasm is infectious, and I love how much of your heart you put into your performance and diving activities."

"Tash, thanks for your leadership of our practice during 2021, especially during a time that I was nowhere near my best. I am grateful for how you kept things going, especially with all the projects that are going to come to fruition in 2022."

The compliment should acknowledge a behaviour in the first instance, and then explain why that made such a difference to you personally.

As an extension of this approach, strengths- and evidence-based compliments can do wonders for a relationship. When was the last time you thanked the people you count on the most for being in your life and supporting you? A strengths-based compliment is fundamentally based in the talent of the person you are delivering the compliment to. What do you notice about them? What are they consistently good at? What do you value them for, even when they aren't intentionally expressing what they are best at? A strengths-based compliment rarely misses the mark, as it usually highlights a behaviour that the recipient has always known they are good at, but never realised that other people have noticed.

For example:

"Antonia, you have an amazing level of energy and creativity that others would only dream of achieving."

"Mom, your thoughtfulness has always brought us closer together, and I am grateful for the love and support you have shown our family over many years."

"Dad, your artistic creativity is inspirational, and I treasure every piece of art you have given us as a connection over many miles and long stretches of time."

THANKING THE FOOD CHAIN

It has been a long time since I have been in any way religious, but one concept I resonate with is the act of saying grace before a meal. From a gratitude point of view, mealtimes are terrific daily moments to be reflective of what you are thankful for in your life. For many, this might only occur once a year at Thanksgiving when people tend to take the time to consciously be thankful for the food they are about to receive.

Whether you take the time to be thankful before a meal, first thing in the morning, or last thing in the evening, it is worth building a habit of gratitude that is easy to fit into your everyday life.

Occasionally, I will get quite introspective about thanking the food chain when considering a meal I am about to eat. For example, who grew the food, who raised the animals (if meat is being consumed), who was in the abattoir, who transported the food, who packed the food, who sold the food in the supermarket, who imported the food (if exotic), who fished the food, who cooked the food, who served the food, who, in the end, has the benefit of eating the food? This process can be applied to any event in a person's life, such as a holiday, a minor or major purchase, and especially an experience. The value of identifying everyone who contributed to an event, purchase, or experience is the ability to offer thanks to those people, even if they never hear it (though many believe on a spiritual level that they will receive your thanks).

HAPPINESS IN AN INSTANT

Let's try an experiment. Right now, on a scale of 1 to 10, how happy are you?

Now, choose a memory, a person, an experience that lifted you up in the past. Focus on that person or that memory – close your eyes and imagine you are with them or back in that experience. Focus on the details; imagine the sounds, the smells, the physical experience. What makes you grateful for that memory or that person in your life? List all the reasons you are grateful.

Now, in this new moment in time, on a scale of 1 to 10, how happy are you?

For most people, this exercise creates a measurable improvement in happiness that is difficult to explain. The endorphins released by the memory lift our experience, and the act of feeling grateful directly translates into a rise in happiness. This strategy can be used at any time, under any circumstance. Whether feeling low and despondent, feeling neutral about life, or feeling good, the process of recollecting a positive person or memory will lift a person's mood almost without fail.

What are your top three positive memories?

Why are you forever grateful for these memories?

How might you use these memories as quick-fire solutions to a low mood?

Consider creating a diary of positive memories in a journal or on a whiteboard. This way, you will always be able to refer back to those moments in time.

THANK YOU FOR PAST, PRESENT, AND FUTURE

Gratitude has an interesting relationship with time. For most, gratitude occurs in the past or the present, when we are feeling thankful for a memory or an experience that occurred today. It is rare for people to build a library of gratitude, with moment after moment logged in appreciation of the experiences that we have participated in. Gratitude journals can be used to serve this purpose, but often, while people take the time to record their thankful moments, they may not take the time to reflect on their journal to identify trends, patterns, or simply to remember the grateful moments they have had the privilege of experiencing.

It may be difficult to explain the relationship between gratitude (for the present or the past) and events in the future. Whether you believe in karma or not, there is a suggestion that our energy in the past and present will deliver our experience in the future. Moments of gratitude during the best and worst parts of our lives have the potential to transform a future into one where our needs, and sometimes our wants, are met, without quite knowing how or why it is happening.

For me, our move from the U.K. to New Zealand falls into this category. There was little rhyme nor reason for our move to the other side of the world, just a feeling of hope and adventure. At the time, we were grateful to be in a financially comfortable enough position to take the calculated risk. With little effort, we found great jobs, a great house, and a great community. I believe our gratitude for having the opportunity to migrate played a big role in the ease with which we set up our new lives. Our move to New Zealand was an example of following your dreams, and it exceeded our expectations. Despite the traumatic events of the last year, I still believe building a life in New Zealand was meant to be, and our life here still has a future to unfold.

Hopes, dreams, goals, and intentions can act as stimuli for future moments of gratitude. Pausing to take stock of what you're most grateful for gives you the ability to build upon these sources as you make a future to be proud of.

As you read this, what future events are you looking forward to feeling grateful for? Who can help you achieve these dreams, and why are you deeply grateful for their assistance or advice?

CHAPTER 11

Of Love and Grief

I wish that heaven had visiting hours
So I could just swing by and ask your advice
What would you do in my situation?
I haven't a clue how I'd even raise them
What would you do? 'Cause you always do
what's right.

Visiting Hours – Ed Sheeran

I T TOOK ME some time, and a lot of pain, to realise that the depth and intensity of grief due to the loss of a loved one is directly proportional to the amount of love you felt for that person when they were alive. The pain is because of how much you loved them, and the importance of the role they played in your life.

THE MULTIPLE EXPRESSIONS OF GRIEF

Grief can be so intense that it causes physical pain in the body, usually in the heart or the gut, but it can show up just about anywhere. Grief can cause crying so long and so intense that you stop breathing. Grief can cause paralysis, and an unwillingness to engage with life even when necessary. Grief can cause confusion and sub-par decision-making, or a hesitancy to make any kind of decision.

The grieving process also takes its toll on relationships. People you thought would stand by you seem to vanish without a word. In contrast, people you never expected show up with a helping hand or a frozen meal when you least expect it. Family and friends struggle to know what to say or how to share their compassion, and they attempt to understand when the situation is not understandable. People sympathise but struggle to empathise; they cannot fathom the scale of loss that you feel.

*How have you expressed grief in the past? Have you **allowed** yourself to express grief that you've needed to feel?*

A great coach once shared with me that grief does not diminish over time, but rather we grow around the grief, which never goes away. Picture a tree, whose roots find a way to grow around an obstacle, absorbing it and making the tree stronger as a result. The earliest months following the loss of a loved one are the most brutal, with many of the symptoms described above appearing and re-appearing. As normal life takes hold, the grief becomes more manageable, though never far from the surface. Different friends and family serve different roles – some talk about the loved one you lost, some talk about everyday issues, some help focus on re-engaging with life and business. Not every conversation helps, but they are all well-intentioned.

Recovery begins to take shape, with capacity to accomplish tasks increasing over time. In the earliest days, it takes gargantuan effort to get out of bed, feed the family, and get the kids to school, and there is no excess energy for anything creative or productive. In time, the days begin to fill with chores around the house and minor administrative tasks. A big breakthrough comes when you have the desire and emotional energy to re-engage with work. I will forever be grateful to my earliest clients following Fiona's passing, who trusted me with their lives and their businesses, all the while giving me permission to be fragile and vulnerable. As time passes, my capacity to work and engage in creative projects is growing, though I have to pace myself as overwhelm creeps up on me. Little triggers can set me back, especially memories of Fiona and her unconditional support for me and the boys. While 2021 was the most terrible year of my life, I am hopeful for a future of new opportunities and future relationships.

LOVE-FISH AND GRIEF-FISH

Love and grief both have the potential to dramatically impact fulfilment, inspiration, success and happiness. Whether defining fulfilment according to a life role or a passion, your love for something or someone in life is likely to feed your sense of purpose. Love also inspires us to take action or create even in the face of significant obstacles, and can lead to unexpectedly positive and extraordinary outcomes. Our love for progress has a huge potential to motivate our success. Feelings of love, or feeling grateful for those we love, has the power to lift our happiness. Even a memory of something or someone we love can bring us happiness.

Throughout the trauma of losing my wife, which took over a year from her first diagnosis to her passing, I was amazed by the low frequency of 0:0:0:0 FISH days, and even the joy of some days that scored a 10 during that journey. Due to the shock and paralysis of the event, the day my wife died absolutely felt like a 0:0:0:0 day. While the days and weeks that followed had the potential to be just as bad or worse, my sense of purpose as a father lifted my fulfilment score above zero fairly often. Indeed, within five days of her passing, I had the joy of watching my sons play and coach basketball, which was a beautiful distraction from recent events. Happiness crept into our lives that day.

Along the way, there were several 10:10:10:10 days – watching my wife swim 150 lengths just after completing her radiotherapy; getting a clear scan five months after her diagnosis, Christmas 2020 as a family, and our holiday in Queenstown in March 2021. These moments made clear to me that a FISH score can be lifted by witnessing or contributing to the success of others, just as easily as creating those achievements yourself.

AROHA ALWAYS

Love seems to surround us in everything we do, and there is no shortage of amazing people willing to lend a hand. Whether life is running smoothly or not, there always seems to be a safety net, usually in the form of a family member or friend keen to help. It takes courage to ask for help, and even more to describe the exact help you most need in that moment. The stress of a crisis and the loss of a loved one can shut down communication and emotions in an unhealthy way. The friends I felt most touched by were those who pushed through and forced me to engage in something as simple as a cup of coffee.

I never fully understood the phrase "Losing the will to live" until I lost Fiona. My love for our boys, and their love for me pulled me through days when I had lost the will to live. This feeling is less wanting to end your life, and more not caring if your life should come to an end, an important distinction. What is clear is that love has the power to heal and the power to rescue people from uncomfortable situations. I will always be grateful for the love that has sustained our family before, during and after Fiona's passing. That love has saved my life more than once.

POWER TO CHANGE THE WORLD

It is no accident that most songs written in music history have love at the heart of their lyrics. Love may be the most powerful force in the Universe and, given its capacity to heal and bring people together, it remains to be seen what love cannot accomplish.

The greatest individuals in human history are characterised by an unexplainable outpouring of love for their life or in their death. Princess Diana, Nelson Mandela, Ruth Bader-Ginsburg, and Mahatma Ghandi were extraordinary in life, and their remarkability was palpable in the outpouring of emotion when they passed. They were all characterised by a level of compassion and understanding for others, even those who were vociferously against what they stood for.

Love has the potential to change the world; in other words, love has the potential to change your world. Giving and receiving love requires a level of vulnerability that is often difficult to achieve if we fail to let our guard down. At the heart of this is our ability to express unconditional love. Can you love someone for who they are, warts and all? Can you love someone regardless of the choices they make in life? More importantly, can you tell someone you love them, no matter what?

What were the top three moments in which you expressed love for someone special?

What were the top three moments in which you received an expression of love from someone special?

How did those moments shape your life?

LOVE VERSUS FEAR

I used to believe that the opposite of love was hate, but I have since realised that fear is a more dangerous enemy to love. Both fear and hate are destructive and toxic to any relationship, and both can be countered by expressions of love in the right circumstance. While hate stirs animosity and anger, fear creates a level of uncertainty that is far more destructive. Hate has the potential to motivate, simply by being against something or someone else. Fear creates paralysis and an inability to make decisions or take action.

Decision making offers a great example of the power of love versus fear. Love offers a level of confidence and certainty to a decision if it is being made in the best interests of everyone it affects (including the decision maker). Even a negative decision can be offered up with love if the intent of the decision maker is one of kindness and compassion. A decision based in love also benefits from the power of certainty and a feeling of what's right considering the available alternatives.

Fear, on the other hand, creates procrastination and uncertainty, with a low level of confidence and feeling unsure about the appropriate direction. A decision founded in fear will often misfire or harm those that the decision affects unintentionally. Other feelings related to fear include anxiety, nervousness or even panic – none of which generally led to good decision making.

What significant decision that you are currently in the throes of making would benefit from a foundation of love?

What fears must you face in order to make some of your pending decisions?

How will your next big decision be founded in love rather than fear?

CONNECTEDNESS

One of love's magical features is its ability to offer unseen connections and opportunities, and alternative paths. It seems that there is no such thing as coincidence and also that everything is a coincidence. Life feels linear, but when we look back at the significant events in one's life, it seems amazing how the Universe conspired to create the path we chose. Most of this is guided by preference, the pursuit of love and the avoidance of pain. My wife often said that the most important decision in someone's life is who they fall in love with. I couldn't agree more, though I am less sure that it is a moment of decision rather than a moment of destiny.

Choices through life are often reflected by the people, places and institutions that we fall in love with, and those we fall out of love with quickly become part of our history as we move on to bigger and better things. Early in life, friendships are formed and broken on the playground as a result of raw emotional intelligence playing itself out. Dating is an early experimentation with romantic love, that eventually leads to a life partner if we are lucky, and the foundations of that relationship are built on all of the previous romantic experiences that we have accumulated.

Life choices such as college/university begin with falling in love with the reputation of the institution you may be interested in, or a particular stream of curriculum that the college is known for, or perhaps a friendship or romantic relationship that draws you to a particular decision. Through our careers, we are likely to make moves based on progress, improved earnings, increases in responsibility or valuing particular organisational cultures (purpose and values) that fit with our own views of the world.

In contrast, exiting a role or organisation is usually preceded by a realisation that there is no 'fit' of purpose and values, or the values are not being lived in an authentic way. In a way, we fall out of love with an employer, and proceed to seek another partner.

What do you love most about your current circumstance?

What do you love least about your current circumstance?

When are you able to be at your best, and when are you at your worst?

Based on the answers to these questions, you should be able to identify a change or no change decision, or even a simple way to improve your current situation. You might simply need to respond differently, or manage emotions with more discipline, rather than making any radical changes.

CHAPTER 12

Beyond FISH, Towards Pure Joy

Everybody is a genius.
But if you judge a fish by its ability to climb a tree,
it will live its whole life believing that it is stupid.

Albert Einstein

T HIS CHAPTER AIMS to explore some of the elements that go beyond FISH. It asks if fulfilment, inspiration, success, and happiness are enough to sustain us.

THE JOY OF FINDING FISHES?

As I wrote this book, it became obvious that although FISH is an important foundation for a life well-lived, it by no means represents everything we need to thrive. Two additional elements feel important to me: **energy** and **strengths**. This realisation led me to consider whether the title of the book should be *The Joy of Finding FISHes*. In the end, the original core of FISH seemed easier to digest, and relevant to most people, especially if you were to begin with tracking your FISH score over time. Six elements just seemed too many to consider, but energy and strengths are important nonetheless, and may represent a future evolution of the FISHes theory.

In the spirit of tracking a FISHes score, here are some questions to consider for the energy and strengths elements:

On a scale of 1 to 10, in the last 24 hours how much energy have you had for all the things you wanted to do?

1   2   3   4   5   6   7   8   9   10

What was the source/cause of your energy score?

_____

_____

_____

On a scale of 1 to 10, in the last 24 hours how able were you to play to your strengths?

1   2   3   4   5   6   7   8   9   10

What were your greatest strengths you leveraged?

_____

_____

_____

SUSTAINING ENERGY

One could argue that building and maintaining sufficient energy to do all the things you wish to accomplish in a day is an important pre-requisite to experiencing fulfilment, inspiration, success, and happiness. I am always amazed at humanity's ability to temporarily ignore the key behaviours for a healthy and energetic lifestyle – good sleep, healthy diet, and exercise being some of the fundamentals. Perhaps if we knew that our Greatest Imaginable Challenge was dependent on good habits, we might have increased motivation to make better lifestyle choices.

It is interesting to reflect on the relationship between energy and fulfilment in the following way:

High Sense of Purpose

Unrealised Potential	Fulfilment / Resilience

Low Energy ← → High Energy

Depression / Despair	Random Action / Exhaustion

Low Sense of Purpose

From the graphic above, it seems obvious that low energy coupled with a low sense of purpose are likely to result in a negative and debilitating frame of mind if sustained over a long period of time. The lack of progress in a person's life, and not being able to do the things they really want to do on a day-to-day basis, will create a downward spiral leading to depression and despair, especially if there is no caring intervention to encourage the person towards a different path.

Low energy coupled with a high sense of purpose creates unrealised potential. In this scenario, an individual may have clear direction or sense of self, but lack the energy (physical, mental, emotional, or spiritual) to create any level of momentum. Think of an elite athlete focused on a world championship title who gets sick prior to the big event. Or a business leader gearing up for a big conference, who has an argument with their spouse just before the delivery. In either case, the individual's well-being let them down and perhaps they were over-preparing or over-training, which may have led to the illness or emotional instability.

High energy and low sense of purpose show up as random actions, which can lead to exhaustion. In this case, an individual has lots of energy but it is completely misdirected and not aligned to a clear direction or purpose at work or in life. Imagine the person who has ten projects on the go, none of which seem to get completed. Productivity and sense of achievement ultimately suffer, and the high energy has the potential to burn out if it all feels for nothing.

Ideally, individuals want to find and sustain a state of high energy and high sense of purpose, even if only for brief periods in their day or week. This state aligns with fulfilment, and the longer it is sustained, the more resilience it will lead to, whereby the individual can hold periods of high energy and high purpose for much longer periods of time.

The model above is intended to demonstrate the value of investing in energy and purpose, and highlight the risks associated with neglecting these states. There may be an argument for non-purposeful rest and recreation time (non-urgent/unimportant activities based on Stephen Covey's urgent/important matrix), but it could be argued that these moments create space from which more purposeful activity can grow.

PLAYING TO STRENGTHS

While I am a strong advocate of Gallup's CliftonStrengths tool, I also believe strengths philosophy has power and relevance whether you use a profiling tool to identify an individual's strengths or not. A simple way to identify strengths and non-strengths would be to consider the following Love Most Matrix:

* What do I love most at work and in life?
* What do I love least?
* What do I do best at work and in life?
* When am I at my worst?

Whether you consider these questions individually or discuss them as a family or with work colleagues, the answers will likely highlight both your natural strengths and the areas to mitigate or avoid if possible. Honest conversations about these questions can shape work and family environments in a way that brings out the best in each individual and lifts happiness on a moment-to-moment basis.

For a more sophisticated approach to strengths-based living and working, consider a tool such as Gallup's CliftonStrengths, which can be accessed here:

https://www.gallup.com/cliftonstrengths/en/252137/home.aspx

This assessment provides a language of 34 themes to describe an individual or team's strengths, which fall into four distinct domains: executing, influencing, relationship building, and strategic thinking. An individual's assessment rarely comes as a surprise, but can be used as a tool for them to become more consciously competent at proactively using strengths to accomplish objectives faster, easier, or with more enjoyment.

What is your number one strength, and how will you leverage this in the future?

As a family, we have the following CliftonStrengths profiles that have helped inform what we love to do most and what we are best at every day:

Christopher	Fiona	Cameron (at age 17)	Ross (at age 12) – Strengths Explorer
Maximiser	Learner	Relator	Dependable
Learner	Harmony	Maximiser	Achieving
Connectedness	Consistency	Strategic	Caring
Input	Responsibility	Command	
Woo	Communication	Achiever	
Positivity	Empathy	Self-Assurance	
Activator	Achiever	Adaptability	
Individualisation	Relator	Woo	
Includer	Positivity	Arranger	
Intellection	Arranger	Competition	
Belief	Woo		
Self-Assurance	Futuristic		
Communication	Developer		
Strategic			
Relator			

The themes above play out regularly in our personal and working lives, and impact our sense of fulfilment, inspiration, success, and happiness. It feels meaningful to remember Fiona by using examples from her list to show how her top strengths underpinned so many of her actions and decisions.

FIVE STRENGTHS OF FIONA

Fiona has always led with **Learner**, which shows up both as a student and as a teacher. Qualifying in law in two different countries (Scotland and New Zealand), training to be a safeguarder and lawyer representing children's views in two different jurisdictions, investing six years of her life in a PhD in law, teaching law, and swimming; she was a student of everything she felt passionate about and the process of learning was a joy to her.

Fiona's **Harmony** exhibited as driving for consensus always, even when none appeared to exist. This theme served her very well as a family lawyer and mediator where she excelled at navigating incredibly challenging situations. Few would believe me if I told them we had a 20-year marriage with no fights or arguments whatsoever. This seems impossible (even to me!) but I credit Fiona's harmony for this.

Consistency in Gallup terms is all about equity and fairness in the way people are treated. For Fiona, this came across as a sense of justice and her passion for representing women and children whose voices were not being heard, which was a cornerstone of her practice as a lawyer. Her PhD topic, consent to medical treatment by individuals under 16 years old, was all about autonomy and fairness in the way parents and health professionals treat young people during their need for health care interventions.

Fiona's **Responsibility** at home and at work was commendable, and the psychological ownership she demonstrated for everything meant that she rarely let anyone down when a promise was made. This theme was one of the reasons she was able to juggle motherhood, practising law, teaching swimming, and completing a PhD simultaneously.

Fiona's **Communication** has always been exceptional, but in her last few years, the quality and eloquence of her written word was extraordinary. Her PhD and subsequent professional articles on related topics all received high praise from professionals with a very discerning eye. In conversation, Fiona was always crystal clear, to the point, and matter of fact, while adding a hint of positivity, fun, and optimism to everything she shared. I miss our conversations and our laughs.

What strengths do you use every single day that make your journey a joyful experience?

How might your strengths help you accelerate the achievement of your Greatest Imaginable Challenge(s)?

How do your strengths reflect what you love to do most and what you do best (in life and at work)?

NON-JUDGEMENTAL, ALWAYS

What I have realised through my coaching and mentoring and through the development of this book is the importance of being non-judgemental toward myself and others in the way we choose to live our lives. There is no right or wrong, just an experience to be acknowledged and observed. Who are we to judge how each topic should be expressed (especially those of fulfilment, inspiration, success, and happiness, which are highly personal)?

I sometimes feel that being non-judgemental towards myself is harder than being non-judgemental towards others. My inner critic feels a need to express itself and challenge my thoughts, speech, and actions in a way that I would never do to others.

Do you find it easy to let go of judgement of others? Do you find it easy to let go of judgement of yourself?

HONOUR THE EVOLUTION

One of my core values is to "Honour the evolution", both for myself and my clients. The spirit of this is to recognise that everyone moves at their own pace and should be respected for doing so. Some of the concepts in this book took years of ruminating before I was able to express foundational elements like core purpose and core values. Clients have taken weeks, months, and in some cases years to mull over ideas like the Greatest Imaginable

Challenge and come out the other side with something meaningful and useful. Ideas take root when we stop putting pressure on ourselves to make decisions quickly or efficiently.

UNDERSTAND OUR HISTORY

Our past behaviour and results will likely inform our future successes. It is worth spending time reflecting on life's great achievements, as these will create a platform from which you can build on future objectives. Our greatest moments may be the result of particular circumstances, expressions of our strengths, leveraging a passion, or being surrounded by the right team of people – all of which could help identify a formula for future success.

Similarly, our past mistakes may provide an indication of the pitfalls to watch out for in the future. For example, if I have a history of procrastinating, and regret missed opportunities, I may wish to address that behaviour or identify the root cause in order to not miss out in the future.

DAYS AT THE EXTREME RE-VISITED

The loss of my wife has provided me with the opportunity to reflect on the best days of our life together. Every day with Fiona was something special. Her life exemplified positivity, adventure, and optimism, and I am grateful to have shared almost exactly 24 years with such an extraordinary person. My most treasured 10:10:10:10 days with Fiona will hold long in my memory. In the final chapter of this book, I have shared some of them, in mostly chronological order, beginning with the day we met.

Navigating the grief associated with the loss of my wife has led to more 0:0:0:0 days in the last three months than the total I'd had prior in my life. Thankfully, my sons and the motivation to be a good dad often pull me out of 0:0:0:0 days. I have faith that I will come through this stronger and with more insight than I probably will know what to do with. For now, it is all about survival.

What needs to happen to experience a 10:10:10:10 day? When was the last one you experienced?

What do you need to do to get yourself out of a 0:0:0:0 day? Who can help you?

CHAPTER 13

A Celebration of Life

We have such a laugh!

Dr Fiona Lindsey Miller

IONA LINDSEY KIRKWOOD and I met on the dancefloor of a Glasgow nightclub, where I had the good fortune of not wearing a ballcap, unlike the friend I had arrived with. Ballcaps on the dancefloor were a negative selection criterion for this discerning Scot! I was in Scotland for the golf Open Championship, visiting from London. Fiona was visiting friends in Glasgow and had travelled through from Edinburgh for the weekend. That night, we danced, immediately connected, and chatted over the loud music of the club nonstop for several hours. That **first** eventful night led to a fabulous weekend in Edinburgh a couple of weeks later and the rest, they say, is history.

For the first five years of our relationship – including over a year of marriage – I lived in the south of England while Fiona lived in Edinburgh. It never seemed strange or difficult for us, as we relished every weekend we spent together, cherished every holiday, and both supported each other in our thriving careers.

My **second** favourite moment was on the eve of the 21st century, the day we got engaged on the esplanade of Edinburgh Castle during a Texas concert. Our engagement nearly didn't happen as planned because Fiona came down with a terrible cold and flu that rendered her bedridden for the day. I was madly rushing around, with the help of her best friend, trying to come up with contingency plans in case Fiona couldn't make the concert. We plied her with medicine and, reluctantly, she dragged herself out into a cold Scottish evening to enjoy a concert of one of her favourite bands. Having been to the same band's concert several months previously, I knew that the opening song would be *Once in a Lifetime*, and took that as my opportunity to ask for

Fiona's hand in marriage. She said yes, and we fail to remember any of the rest of the concert!

My **third** favourite day was our wedding day, which was one of the most joyful and memorable days for us both. Family and friends travelled from near and far, and we were married in St Giles' Cathedral on the Royal Mile in Edinburgh, followed by the reception at the Balmoral. Highlights for me were watching Fiona enter through the cathedral doors with a snowstorm framing her in the doorway; her smile, laughter, and her signature cartwheel on the dancefloor that evening. The night ended with me and Fiona alone in Palm Court Bar at the Balmoral at 3a.m., chatting about what an extraordinary day it had been.

My **fourth** and **fifth** favourite days were the births of Cameron and Ross in 2003 and 2008. Cameron's birth in Glasgow was highly stressful, due to medical challenges affecting both Fiona and Cameron that day. Each challenge was navigated successfully, and the relief after the birth for all of us as a family was palpable. Many people don't realise that during her pregnancy with Cameron, Fiona was terrified of becoming a mother. Ironically, she was not sure she was up to the responsibility and was worried she would not live up to her own expectations. From day one, Cameron put her and us at ease. If we ever had any nerves, Cameron would always show us the way; he brought himself up in many ways!

Ross' birth was far less complicated and stressful. We were excited to bring a new Kiwi into the world in Wellington. My greatest memory from that day was phoning Cameron, who was with his grandparents at Wellington Zoo. In their excitement to answer our call, the mobile phone nearly fell down the drain, and Cameron nearly lost his opportunity to hear the exciting news!

The boys have been the very best things to have happened to us in our 24 years together. They have brought an enormous amount of joy and pride, from sporting achievements to concerts, and family laughs around the dinner table to memorable holidays around the world. Cameron and Ross are Fiona's legacy, and they will always do her proud.

My **sixth** favourite moment with Fiona took place during one of her many Greatest Imaginable Challenges. The year we decided to immigrate to New Zealand, my wife woke up one morning and casually declared, "I know what I am going to do before we move to New Zealand... I am going to cycle the length of Great Britain!". I think my response was, "That's nice, dear, let me know if you will need any help with that!". Fiona then took it upon herself to train, do a trial run from Edinburgh to St Andrews, plan the route, book the accommodation, and coax me and Cameron (then three years old) to be her support crew.

We drove from Edinburgh to Land's End in Cornwall and one bright sunny morning Fiona set off on her journey, all by herself. I never felt so proud and daunted for her at the same time. For seventeen days, Cameron and I dropped her off at her starting point and picked her up at the end of the day when she finished. While her departure was significant, and her finish at John O'Groats in the northeast of Scotland memorable, my favourite moment of the entire journey was when she cycled over the border from England into Scotland. That moment symbolised coming home, and made me certain, with two thirds of the journey completed, that she would finish no matter what. Her determination and ability to fulfil an intention were legendary.

While physical challenges were right up her alley, she never shied away from an intellectual challenge either. Everything in her history was simply a warmup to Fiona's greatest academic achievement, the pursuit of a PhD in law. This six-year adventure was managed part-time, while working full time as a lawyer, part-time as a swimming teacher, and thriving as a wife and mother. Fuelled by her history as a child advocate, Fiona chose to build her PhD on the topic of the consent of minors to medical and surgical treatment. Fiona's commitment to helping children have their voices heard was at the heart of her research and her life.

She had exceptional supervisors for her endeavour, and their summary of Fiona's academic journey does far better justice than I ever could. What is remarkable is not that she undertook such a challenge – she was always up for it – nor that she completed the PhD – her determination would never let her fail – but that she spent six years enjoying every single minute. From the comparative legal systems, to interviews with children and health professionals, to the writing, and the editing, and shaping her insights and conclusions, not one moment felt like hard work. We laughed that the hardest part about the whole process was the administration required for the online submission of her thesis. Everything else was a breeze for my extraordinary wife.

My **seventh** memorable moment, therefore, was Fiona's graduation day in Dunedin as we celebrated the completion of her PhD. Pipe-band procession, kilts, gowns, caps, conferring of a massive degree, and a celebratory dinner out all combined to create a fitting conclusion to six years of hard work.

My **eighth** favourite day in Fiona's life happened every Tuesday evening for the last several years. Tuesday nights saw Fiona invest in her favourite job, by far: that of a swimming teacher. She had been a swimming teacher since she was a teenager and, through thick and thin, maintained her credentials and practised teaching stroke techniques throughout her life. Tuesday nights at Khandallah School pool was where Fiona got some of the most joy outside our home. She never failed to come home beaming, laughing, or singing the praises of all her adult students, and forever exclaiming, "We have such a laugh!".

My **ninth** favourite day happened the year we got married. Fiona's dream to see New Zealand was realised over Christmas of 2001, when we saw the country from Cape Rienga to Milford Sound. Fiona's adventurous spirit was truly put to the test when we arrived in Queenstown. We woke up early to a beautiful sunrise over the mountains and proceeded in a rickety van along a one-way track beside a steep embankment to the headwaters of one of the surrounding rivers. We spent the morning rafting and bodysurfing through the most incredible rapids. To recover, we then found our way to Gibston Valley Estate for a wine tour and lovely lunch. Fortuitously, Gibston Valley is not that far away from the home of AJ Hacket's original bungee experience. Fiona and I both threw ourselves off the Kawarau Bridge, and one of us took a dip in the river below! The day was still young, so we proceeded up a mountain, strapped ourselves to a guide and a hang-glider, and floated down to the valley below. We celebrated the day with a Mexican feast and lots of reminiscing about what an amazing day we had enjoyed together.

Skip ahead 19 years, and the Miller family attempted to recreate that glorious day in Queenstown! Only this time, Fiona and I were spectators and our boys were the adventurers. They each did a bungee on Fiona's 53rd birthday, and we celebrated as a family at the top of the gondola where the boys also enjoyed a luge ride. That recent trip to Queenstown gave us some of the last and most beautiful pictures of Fiona and of us as a family. It is my **tenth** favourite memory.

One of Fiona's many talents was anticipating what our family needed, collectively and individually. The most recent example was her excitement, between brain surgeries, to invest in a fifth member of our family. Within a window of about eight weeks, when Fiona was at her strongest, she spontaneously searched for Vizsla puppies and convinced me that although we had planned on a dog in retirement, there was absolutely no reason why we couldn't bring the decision forward, and that now was the time! A few weeks before the diagnosis of Fiona's recurring brain tumour, Ross and I spent two days travelling to the Waikato and back to pick up Talisker, our crazy and beautiful puppy. Deep down, I believe Fiona knew that we would need Tali to comfort us and keep us busy, both during Fiona's decline and after her passing. Every day, I am grateful that we added Tali to the family.

Fiona was extraordinary on every level – as a parent, as a wife, as a best friend. She approached each day with a positive spirit and an enthusiasm that was infectious. I have struggled since she left to know what to do or what decisions to make. Two questions help me remember which direction to take:

1) What would Fiona do?
   (When I get up from laughing at the fact that it would probably involve a somersault, a cartwheel, or juggling, I ask my second question.)
2) What would Fiona want me to do?

In her heart, she would want us all to do our best and have fun. That is what she lived for.

Epilogue

WHEN CHAPTER 1 was completed, Fiona had just undergone her second brain surgery. While we considered a variety of additional interventions, none appeared to have a strong enough benefit-risk ratio and quality of life profile to warrant proceeding. Fiona's surgery probably bought us a few months of mobility and freedom during the first half of 2021. Most significantly, Fiona was well enough to travel to Queenstown in March for a family holiday that none of us will soon forget. Magical sunrises, bungee jumps, luge rides, and a variety of delicious places to eat filled our four days, along with a lot of smiles and laughter.

Unfortunately, Fiona's health deteriorated through the month of April, and her mobility became highly restricted moving into May, when she was admitted to in-patient care with Mary Potter Hospice in Wellington. Fiona became progressively bed-ridden, with occasional trips in the cloud-chair out on the terrace where we sang and reminisced. Her hospice stay was characterised by exceptional care and good friends spending quality time with her in her final months.

Early July saw Cameron and Ross travel to Auckland to compete in the National Diving Championships. It felt very emotional and surreal as I received and forwarded video clips of the boys diving to friends and family around the world, all the while being with Fiona as she slowly slipped away.

One of the doctors at the hospice shared with me her view that as a person dies, they determine the timing and circumstances of their passing. The boys and I were prepared for many scenarios, but we believed Fiona would likely pass away on her own, for the sheer autonomy of the situation. It was remarkable how, in her final day, she waited for us all to be together, and took her last breath as I held her hand and the boys were sitting with me nearby. This was the saddest day of my life.

The months following her passing felt brutal and my grief was painful and physical, as I outline in Chapter 11. I am slowly growing around my grief. It will never disappear, but I can grow stronger around and through it. It took several months after Fiona's passing to feel inspired to write again, but the final four chapters took shape in the last few months of 2021.

At the outset, I set out to write a positive and optimistic story, filled with practical tools and questions to help anyone build the life of their dreams. The final result is rather rawer than that; it is a balance of optimism and realism in the face of huge obstacles. I hope that this honesty benefits all who read it, as you will have your own great challenges in your life. Having explored various facets of fulfilment, inspiration, success, and happiness, I look forward to a future dominated by pure joy.

Fiona lived by the value that "Life is fun and easy". I am going to spend the rest of my life trying to live up to her expectation.

Cover me in sunshine
Shower me with good times
Tell me that the world's been spinning since
the beginning
And everything will be alright
Cover me in sunshine!

P!nk, Willow Sage Hart

WORK WITH ME

I am always on the lookout for great people who value investing in their lives or their businesses in the pursuit of excellence.

While most of my clients are based in New Zealand, video technology has opened up new markets, including Australia and North America.

Typically, I offer the following coaching and mentoring services:

* Strengths-based strategic planning and business coaching to small-business owners (fewer than 10 employees).
* Work-life integration coaching to any business leader struggling with balance in their life.
* Mentoring for Gallup-Certified CliftonStrengths coaches seeking to set up or grow their own coaching practices.
* The Business of Strengths-Based Healthcare programme for private sector health professionals (physiotherapists, dentists, chiropractors, etc.).

With the publication of *The Joy of Finding FISH*, I am also keen to support anyone seeking more fulfilment, inspiration, success, and happiness in their lives!

Please reach out to me at **chris@christophermiller.co.nz** to discuss how we might work together.

ABOUT THE AUTHOR

Christopher had the great privilege of being born on Canada Day in Halifax, Nova Scotia in 1971. Growing up in a Navy family, he had the opportunity to live in a variety of cities across Canada and in the United Kingdom.

Christopher earned a BScH in Life Sciences from Queen's University in Kingston and went on to complete an MBA in Health Services Management from McMaster University in Hamilton, where he was nominated valedictorian for his graduating class.

Upon graduation from McMaster, Christopher moved to London and began a career in the pharmaceutical industry. Following one and a half years of sales experience in East London, Christopher joined the marketing team at Schering Health Care Ltd and became product manager for their wide range of contraception products including Microgynon, Femodene, Mirena IUS, and Levonelle, the U.K.'s first over-the-counter emergency contraceptive pill. During this period of his career, Christopher married Fiona, his best friend and confidante, in 2001.

Following marketing management roles with Invitrogen (biotechnology) and Pfizer (local marketing manager for Northern Ireland), Christopher and his family immigrated to New Zealand where he joined Results.com, a national business-coaching company specialising in small businesses. Christopher managed a portfolio of up to 14 clients per week for a period of three years with Results. He then joined Gallup, a global management consultant company where, as Senior Consultant, he managed all of Gallup's employee engagement and CliftonStrengths culture change programmes throughout New Zealand, while supporting a select few Australian clients.

In September 2017, Christopher set up his own coaching and mentoring practice where he supports small-business owners, CliftonStrengths coaches and health care practices in their pursuit of exceptional businesses and lives.

Christopher lives in Wellington, New Zealand with his two sons, Cameron and Ross. When he is not helping clients in their businesses or lives, he is often found at the Wellington Regional Aquatic Centre where he cheers on the local springboard and platform diving club.

Reader Praise for
The Joy of Finding FISH
A Journey of Fulfilment, Inspiration, Success and Happiness

The chapter on gratitude brought me so much hope and promise, especially as I knew what Chris was going through during the time that he wrote this chapter. Despite whatever our life circumstances may be, the practice of finding something to be thankful for makes even the tiniest things grow into something bigger in our lives. Being joyful isn't what makes you grateful; being grateful is what makes you joyful. The mere 'practice' of gratitude is a way of reflecting on what's most important in our lives - past, present and future. Simply noticing the specific details in others that I'm grateful for, and telling them these things, is a way of sharing these microscopic seeds and growing them into something bigger. I believe it's all of our jobs to be the gardeners of our own lives, making sure we tend to and water our own plants and those around us – the practice of gratitude helps us do just this.

— Antonia Milkop, Strengths Coach & Facilitator, AntoniaMilkop.com

Whilst you can see yourself within the Joy of Finding FISH chapters, Chapter 4 helps curate what this looks like for oneself and the bespoke pathways we each take. Powerful questions, revelation insights and relatable anecdotes help focus the lens of reflection on starting to make tangible steps today to create a life that makes me proud.

— Natasha Nihill, Business Development Manager

Chris is able to break down the concept of creating Purpose and Values in a way that doesn't feel like a 'pressure cooker' situation to 'get it right' or think they aren't 'big enough'. He also helps you identify, if you already have values, why you may not feel aligned or are in conflict with them.

Drawing on his own past experiences and client examples, Chris easily steps you through a no-pressure framework for answering those bigger 'why's' you may have. With thought-provoking questions and references, you realise that there is no right or wrong to this important step to achieving fulfilment, just you. You are able to walk away with a clearer vision of your individual journey, why, purpose and values.

— Frankie Jago, Video Marketing Strategist, Get Ahead Media

Chris's words and teachings are legitimised by the journey he has navigated to mean them. He is his and this book's lived truth. Through tragedy and love, chaos and clarity, upheaval and centre, Chris has developed his teachings to a profound level of understanding. I recommend this book to anyone looking for any semblance of clarity in any area of their life.

— Kate Wilson, Adjudicator

CPSIA information can be obtained
at www.ICGtesting.com
Printed in the USA
LVHW070454220622
721766LV00010B/406